I remember my first acquaintance v
Apologetics class at *Faculté de théolc*
me as a very able young man but I h
Theology. Then, in 2004, he registered in my Homiletics class. I was amazed at
the change that took place in him in such a short period of time. He was constantly
interrupting me, asking all kinds of questions; obviously, his heart was entirely in
the things of the Kingdom. In fact, through his constant intervention, he
contributed to transform my Homiletics class into a Pastoral Theology class.

It is during that period that he approached me one night, asking me to be his
mentor. It really caught me by surprise, but I joyfully accepted. It has been the
beginning of a most blessed friendship, so much so, that I came to consider him as
a son.

Then came this master of Theology project in which I acted as a study supervisor.
When Pascal first came to me with his dissertation topic, I was not sure where he
was heading. But as months went by, I became more and more enthusiastic with
the specifics of the subject as well as with his treatment of it.

Needless to say that the subject could not have been more timely as Covenant
Theology is gaining ground among Evangelical Protestantism. When I came to an
understanding of Covenant Theology, about three decades ago, it appeared to me
as the most coherent and consistent interpretative framework for Scripture. It is
not a new concept for we can trace the idea of covenant from the Early Church.
And it is an approach that occupied our forefathers at the time of the Reformation.
Its importance comes also from the fact that no doctrine exists in isolation with the
others; all doctrines are in some way related. Thus, more specifically, Covenant
Theology impacts our doctrines of the Church and of Baptism.

Historically, Puritans were holding to Covenant Theology, though there were
some differences in their understanding of the biblical covenants. And it is
precisely at this point that Reformed Credobaptists and Paedobaptists disagree,
whence their divergences on the doctrines of the Church and Baptism.

In order to grasp the subtleties of a doctrine, it is of great importance to look at its
development, how the data of Scripture have been processed and where some
shifts have taken place. This is the analysis that makes up the content of Pascal's
dissertation that is here presented in this book. One cannot but be impressed with
the clarity of his compelling arguments, the careful and wise selection of his
documentation and the irenic spirit in which he has written. As he brings us back
to some of the seventeenth-century writings, we cannot help but ask ourselves
why these precious and sound works have fallen into oblivion.

Whether one agrees or disagrees with Pascal's arguments and conclusion, nobody can read this book without admitting the seriousness and the soundness of the facts that are reported and that make it a most commendable book on the subject.

According to Pascal's own words, one of his desires in writing this book was *to breathe new life into the debates of seventeenth- century theologians.* After reading it, we can certainly say: Mission accomplished.

Raymond Perron Ph.D
Église réformée baptiste de la Capitale
Quebec city, Qc

****

This book by Pascal Denault is a welcome addition to the literature on an issue that has vexed many for too long. It is clear that the seventeenth-century Particular Baptists' formulation of covenant theology in the Second London Confession of Faith—1677/89 (cf. 2nd LCF 7.3, for example) was a modified version of the one contained in the Westminster Confession of Faith. But why the different formulation? Denault's work goes *ad fontes* (to the sources) to find the answer. And that's exactly why I am so thankful for his work. The primary, Particular Baptist sources are where we should start in seeking to understand the theology of our forebears. Denault shows from those sources not only *that* the Baptist formulation of covenant theology differed but *why*. It is too easy to note that it differed and then to impose our thought categories upon the Confession to answer the question of why. That is poor scholarship and bad historical-theological method. Denault's method is sound and a much-needed tonic in our day of rediscovering our roots. His findings are illuminating and will challenge many. He argues that the main difference had nothing to do with the covenant of works. The Particular Baptists were of one voice with their paedobaptist brethren on this issue. Neither did the main difference focus on the subjects of baptism, though it was a related issue. The main difference, according to Denault (and I think he is right), had to do with their view of covenant theology, concentrating on the definition of the covenant of grace and the differences between the old and new covenants in light of that definition.

Denault calls Nehemiah Coxe "the most significant Baptist theologian [of the seventeenth century] when it comes to Covenant Theology." He is surely right. Coxe wrote a treatise on the covenants from Adam through Abraham and was, most likely, a co-editor of the 2nd LCF. So any attempt to understand our Confession must start with Coxe and the context in which he wrote. This is what Denault does for us.

It is of interest to note that Coxe did not write on the differences between the old and new covenants due to the publication of John Owen's exposition of Hebrews 8:6-13. The old Baptists agreed with much of Owen's work (and the work of other paedobaptists on this issue). However, they differed with Owen and others on other points. Denault's work reveals to us what those other points were and how they argued from covenant theology to credobaptism.

I heartily commend this work to all Reformed Baptist pastors (and all others interested in covenant theology). Brothers, this is a must-read. As a Reformed Baptist pastor myself, I remember the first time I read seventeenth-century covenant theology from a Baptist perspective. It was both challenging and refreshing. It challenged me to rethink how covenant theology ought to be formulated and it refreshed me on two levels. First, it gave me a sound system of doctrine that reflected the teachings of Scripture from creation to consummation. Second, it helped me understand our Confession better. May this work do the same for many others!

Richard C. Barcellos, Ph.D.
Grace Reformed Baptist Church
Palmdale, CA

****

Pascal Denault deserves many thanks for his labor in researching and describing the nuances of English covenant theology in the Seventeenth Century. He has uncovered significant factors contributing to the differences between Presbyterian and Particular Baptist thought and practice, describing theological categories in easily accessible terms. He shows that in the formulations of covenant theology, the two groups had both similarities and significant divergences. For example, he shows that the facile popular notion that the Baptists scrupled over the concept of a Covenant of Works in their Confession is utterly false; in fact, they agreed in every way with their paedobaptist counterparts on this issue. But they differed on the nature of the revelation and administration of the Covenant of Grace. This drove their ecclesiology and their practice of credobaptism. This is an important work and deserves wide circulation.

James M. Renihan, Ph.D.
Dean, Professor of Historical Theology
Institute of Reformed Baptist Studies

****

It is with great pleasure that I recommend this Master's thesis of Pastor Pascal Denault. Pastor Denault has identified the primary difference between a Presbyterian covenant theology and a Reformed Baptist covenant theology which ultimately leads to their respective doctrine of the church and the sacraments. With many references to original sources in the 17th Century, he shows that the Presbyterian concept of the Covenant of Grace relies upon a substance/administration hermeneutic which leads to the "one covenant under two administrations (OT/NT)" structure. This structure allows the Presbyterian to transfer the organic element of "believers and their seed" from the Abrahamic/Sinai Covenant administration into the New Covenant administration, thus allowing a mixed church of believers and unbelievers as well as infant baptism corresponding to circumcision. Further, he shows that the Reformed Baptist construction of the Covenant of Grace was established by a "revealed/concluded" (promise/fulfillment) structure, progressively revealed in the OT by "the covenants of the promise" and concluded in the NT by the institution of the New Covenant as the promise of the Covenant of Grace fulfilled. This is the primary difference between the covenant theologies of the Westminster Confession and the 1689 Second London Baptist Confession.

With rich quotations from original Presbyterian and Baptist resources in the 17th Century (worth the cost of the book alone), Pastor Denault shows that the Baptists agreed on their revealed/concluded structure with John Owen, although he remained a paedobaptist. His thesis is that Baptists carried out their same structure as Owen's to the end by establishing "the baptism of disciples alone" in a confessor's church model, contrary to the Presbyterians. His final conclusion is that the Presbyterian commitment to infant baptism affected their reluctance to adopt the Baptist "revealed/concluded" model over the "one covenant under two administrations" model, whether consciously or unconsciously.

The value of this work is that it clarifies the difference between the Presbyterian and Baptist models of the Covenant of Grace, adequately defending the Baptist model as well as clarifying the Baptist model as a basis to unify differences between Baptists on covenant theology today. I pray that this work will contribute to the raising up of more Reformed Covenantal Baptist churches which avoid the errors of Dispensationalism, Theonomy, the Federal Vision, and law/gospel errors. It is worthy to be read by all concerned.

Fred A. Malone, Ph.D.
Author of *The Baptism of Disciples Alone*
First Baptist Church of Clinton, LA

****

The beauty of covenant theology is that it provides the biblical student with a comprehensive and cohesive covenantal framework of the history of redemption. This is important, because both comprehensiveness and cohesiveness are vital for any biblical system of thought: especially for a doctrinal system that seeks to explain the relationship between the various covenants of the Old and New Testament. Pascal Denault not only shows the historical distinctives between seventeenth century Presbyterian and Baptist covenant theology, but he also explains that the early framers of Baptist Federalism understood the inconsistency of placing the Mosaic Covenant into the covenant of grace. This inconsistency causes Paedobaptist Covenant Theology to break down upon its own weight. According to Pascal, the Federalism of the early Baptists was not identical to Presbyterian Federalism, minus infant baptism, but a more biblical and pure covenantal system that is comprehensive, cohesive and self-supporting. Pascal goes on to faithfully elucidate the covenantal view of the early Baptist by making accessible a vast amount of research on the primary sources. Not only do I think that this is an excellent and valuable resource, I believe it is one of the best upon this subject. This is such an informative and helpful book that I pray that our covenant Lord providentially places this book into the hands of every student of covenant theology.

Jeffrey D. Johnson
Author of *The Fatal Flaw of the Theology Behind Infant Baptism*

****

Pascal Denault's careful labors over the theological texts of both Baptists and Paedobaptists of the seventeenth century have yielded an excellent study of the relation of baptism to a commonly shared covenantalism. At the same time he has shown that a distinct baptistic interpretation of the substance of the New Covenant, that is, all its conditions having been met in the work of Christ its Mediator resulting in an unconditional application of it to its recipients, formed the most basic difference between the two groups. His careful work on the seventeenth-century documents has yielded a strong, Bible-centered, covenantal defense of believers' baptism and is worthy of a dominant place in the contemporary discussions of both covenantalism and baptism.

Thomas J. Nettles, Ph.D.
Professor of Historical Theology
The Southern Baptist Theological Seminary

****

The issue of the relationship between the Old and New Covenants is not a new one. It is as old as Christianity, but has become something of a "hot potato" especially since the Puritan era. That period in Christian history saw the emergence of the Baptists from the Puritan matrix, and while the Baptists shared much in common with their Puritan forebears, they disagreed with their parents and brothers in the Faith on this issue of how the New Covenant related to the Old. This new study by Pascal Denault is most helpful in providing an accurate summary of the historic discussion between the Baptists and their fellow Puritans, and then showing the way this discussion bears on the contemporary treatment of a vital issue.

Michael A.G. Haykin, Th.D.
Professor of Church History & Biblical Spirituality
The Southern Baptist Theological Seminary

****

The Distinctiveness of Baptist Covenant Theology

Other Solid Ground Titles on This Subject

In addition to the work you hold in your hands, Solid Ground is honored to have also published the following titles on this subject:

COVENANT THEOLOGY: *A Reformed and Baptistic Perspective on God's Covenants* by Greg Nichols

"Baptists who embrace their historic Calvinistic and Covenantal roots have long since needed a robust and comprehensive treatment of Covenant Theology that includes the nuanced interpretations of the biblical covenants that a baptistic hermeneutic requires. This treatment by Greg Nichols does just that and more. As a devotee of the Westminster tradition (including its chapter, 'On God's Covenant with Man'), I differ here and there; sometimes significantly so. But there is so much to applaud in this volume and Baptists will do well to read this volume carefully and with much gratitude. A splendid achievement. I, for one, will insist that my Presbyterian students read it." - **Derek W. H. Thomas**

"There has been an urgent need for Reformed Baptists to produce a work on the covenants. I am so thankful that Greg Nichols has engaged this very weighty work. It is a very timely addition on a vitally important topic and adds much to a growing Reformed Baptist literary body." - **James R. White**

COVENANT THEOLOGY: *A Baptist Distinctive*
edited by Earl Blackburn

"In the 20th Century, a minimalist theological climate developed among Baptists. Fighting for the fundamentals of the faith tended to reduce the importance of detailed confessional statements making only a few core doctrines central to Baptist identity. This modest doctrinal focus was stoutly defended by noble men, but in reducing Christian theology to a few essentials, they opened the door for a new structural system 'Dispensationalism' to overwhelm the older covenantalism of the Baptist churches and Confessions. Only in the later decades of the century has there been an attempt to recover the framework that was lost. This book is a helpful addition to the growing body of literature that demonstrates the centrality of covenantalism to Baptist life and practice. It will be very useful to assist in the recovery of our understanding of the older and more Scriptural system." - **James M. Renihan**

The Distinctiveness
of Baptist Covenant Theology

*A Comparison Between Seventeenth-Century
Particular Baptist and Paedobaptist Federalism*

Pascal Denault

Solid Ground Christian Books
Birmingham, Alabama USA

Solid Ground Christian Books
PO Box 660132
Vestavia Hills AL 35266
205-443-0311
mike.sgcb@gmail.com
www.solid-ground-books.com

The Distinctiveness of Baptist Covenant Theology
A Comparison Between Seventeenth-Century Particular Baptist and Paedobaptist Federalism

First Solid Ground Edition—January 2013

*Special thanks to Guy Leroux for his excellent cover design.

ISBN- 978-159925-325-1

Translated from French by Mac and Elizabeth Wigfield

Summary

This position paper deals with covenant theology. This approach to Scripture was born of the Protestant Reformation and was developed extensively thereafter, particularly by the seventeenth-century Puritans. Covenant theology is the foundation of reformed thinking as outlined in the Westminster Confession of Faith (1646).

There was a consensus at the heart of reformed Puritanism concerning the doctrines of revelation, of the Trinity, of divine sovereignty, of the fall and man's sin, of the grace of God, of the person and the work of Christ and, to some degree, of the law. There were, however, important disagreements regarding the doctrine of the Church as well as that of baptism. These two doctrines could not be considered in isolation because they had basic theological implications. These implications are what we call covenant theology. The fact that the Puritans had different views on the Church and on baptism is the result of a different way of understanding biblical covenants.

The seventeenth-century Puritans can be divided into three groups: Presbyterians, Congregationalists and Baptists. The first two groups were paedobaptists while the third was credobaptist. The divide with regard to covenant theology was caused by the issue of baptism. The paedobaptists defended one understanding of covenant theology and the Baptists defended another. The aim of this study is to present and compare these two distinct approaches side by side. We wish to breathe new life into the debates of seventeenth-century theologians' by using their own writings. As much as possible, we will attempt to define the characteristics of paedobaptist and Baptist theologies to give the reader a clear idea of that which distinguishes these two groups.

The introduction will further develop the usefulness of the hypothesis which states that covenant theology is the fundamental distinction upon which all of the other differences between Presbyterians and Baptists are built. After a brief overview of the development of covenant theology, we will examine the sources used for this work.

Chapter 1 explains how the reformers understood the Covenant of Works. This chapter is much shorter since the vital divergence between the two theologies that are the subject of this thesis was not found at this level. The second chapter, about the Covenant of Grace is the longest since it presents the foundation of paedobaptist and Baptist belief. We will discover two radically different ways of thinking that support two distinct theologies. Each conception of the Covenant of Grace had hermeneutic and theological consequences that we will examine.

The last two chapters, about the Old and New Covenants, are based on Chapter 2. The Covenant of Grace determined the way that the other biblical covenants were understood by Presbyterians and Baptists alike. Since most of the considerations and the issues surrounding the New Covenant are broached in Chapter 2, the chapter on the Old Covenant is longer. This chapter covers the Abrahamic Covenant in relation to the Covenant of Grace and the Mosaic Covenant. We will see, for the most part, how Baptists rejected the Presbyterian understanding of this covenant and how they replaced it. The chapter also deals with the Mosaic Covenant, its nature and how it relates to the Covenant of Works as well as the New Covenant. The chapter on the New Covenant is limited to the matter of its newness. This is done by respectively applying the paedobaptist and Baptist paradigms of the Covenant of Grace. The consequences of one theological model versus the other become apparent when they are applied to the New Covenant.

By the end of this study, the reader should have a clear understanding of the foundational distinctives which exist between paedobaptist and Baptist theologies and where they respectively culminate.

Table of Contents

Preface and Acknowledgements 1

INTRODUCTION...5
  1. HYPOTHESIS 5
  2. METHODOLOGY AND ORIGINAL SOURCES..................8
    2.1. Confessions of faith and catechisms 9
    2.2. Paedobaptist and Baptist theologians........................11
      2.2.1. The Paedobaptists 11
      2.2.2. The Baptists..14
    2.3. John Owen the Baptist 18
  3. BRIEF HISTORICAL OVERVIEW OF COVENANT
    THEOLOGY 23

CHAPTER 1 THE COVENANT OF WORKS.....................27
  1. DESCRIPTION AND FUNCTION OF THE COVENANT OF
    WORKS 27
  2. THE RELATIONSHIP BETWEEN THE COVENANT OF
    WORKS AND THE OLD COVENANT...............................30

CHAPTER 2 THE COVENANT OF GRACE.....................35
  1. THE COVENANT OF GRACE IN THE SEVENTEENTH
    CENTURY..35
    1.1. Socianism and the Covenant of Grace 36
  2. THE COVENANT OF GRACE AS SEEN BY THE
    PAEDOBAPTISTS: ONE COVENANT UNDER TWO
    ADMINISTRATIONS..39
    2.1. A fundamental distinction between the substance and
    the administration..39
    2.2. From the "one covenant under two administrations"
    model to the principle of succession 44
    2.3. One covenant under two administrations: a generalized
    Model 48

3. THE COVENANT OF GRACE AS SEEN BY BAPTISTS: A COVENANT REVEALED PROGRESSIVELY AND FORMALLY CONCLUDED 55
  3.1. Unity above all 55
  3.2. Rejection of the Presbyterian model 58
  3.3. The affirmation of the Baptist model 61
    3.3.1. The Covenant of Grace revealed Progressively 61
    3.3.2. The Covenant of Grace fully revealed in the New Covenant 63
    3.3.3. The Covenant of Grace and the Old Covenant 68
    Summary 74
4. A FEW COMPARISONS BETWEEN THESE TWO MODELS 78
  4.1. The hermeneutical comparisons 78
  4.2. The theological comparisons 83
    4.2.1. The Way to Enter Into the Covenant of Grace 83
    4.2.2. The Range and Effectiveness of Grace in the Covenant of Grace 88
    4.2.3. The Unconditional Nature of the Covenant of Grace 95
CONCLUSION 96

CHAPTER 3 THE OLD COVENANT 99
1. WHAT DOES THE EXPRESSION "OLD COVENANT" MEAN? 99
  1.1. The Cumulative Aspect of the Old Covenant 99
  1.2. A Difficulty for the Paedobaptists 101
    1.2.1. Solution 1: the Mosaic Covenant was Unconditional 102
    1.2.2. Solution 2: the Mosaic Covenant was distinct from the Covenant of Grace and concluded with Abraham 111
2. THE ABRAHAMIC COVENANT 115

2.1. The duality of the Abrahamic Covenant 117
    2.1.1. Two posterities and two covenants in
        Abraham 119
    2.1.2. The intertwining of the two posterities under
        the Old Covenant 125
3. THE MOSAIC COVENANT 129
    3.1. The goal of the Old Covenant 130
    3.2. The nature of the Old Covenant 134
CONCLUSION AND SUMMARY 141

CHAPTER 4 THE NEW COVENANT 145
    1. THE NEWNESS OF THE NEW COVENANT 145
        1.1. The unconditional nature of the New Covenant 148
        1.2. The substance of the New Covenant 153

CONCLUSION 155

BIBLIOGRAPHY 157

Preface and Acknowledgments

The Baptists, in stride with the separatist Puritans of the sixteenth century and seventeenth century in England, rejected the Presbyterianism directly inherited from the Geneva Reformation according to the teachings of John Calvin. However, these same Baptists called themselves Calvinists. What distinguished a Presbyterian Calvinist from a Baptist Calvinist? You will understand that this is a crucial question for someone who named his sons Calvin and Baptiste respectively. The short answer to this question is baptism. The long answer is the theology that implies baptism: covenant theology. In this position paper, we will study the long answer by comparing two very different ways of understanding covenant theology in the seventeenth century: the main-stream understanding of the Presbyterians who were paedobaptists and the unconventional understanding of the Baptists who refused to baptize children and practised baptism for believers.

The writing of this dissertation would not have been possible without the invaluable support and help of several people whom I wish to thank. First of all, I would like to thank my beloved brothers and sisters from the Église Évangélique de St-Jérôme who paid dearly for the theology which will be presented in these pages by becoming a Reformed Baptist church. I was to start this work of research as of 2007 to obtain a master's degree in theology. I planned on it being a quick and easy project. By the winter of 2009, I still had nothing done being too occupied with my other obligations. It was at that point my church decided to free me from my pastoral duties for four months so that I could devote myself completely to this project. I spent weeks communing with seventeenth-century theologians through their writings; sometimes reading them with a magnifying glass when only the original edition existed. By the end of the four months, I had not yet started writing; but I knew what I was going to say. It took me a little more than another year to finish. During all that time, the church supported me unconditionally through prayers and often through help in our home, allowing me to work in greater peace. Today I am touched and sincerely thankful when I think of the love you have shown me. Being united with you in the New Covenant is an immense joy and serving you, an honour.

I want to thank Caroline, my wife, with whom I am discovering the promises and obligations of a life of covenant. Your perseverance with me in this endeavour has been of great comfort to me and a concrete manifestation of your love for me, for our home and, above all else, for Him who loved us first.

A special word of thanks is also due to Dr. Raymond Perron who has been not only a thesis advisor but a true pastor. Thank you for your constant encouragement which was a genuine source of motivation to keep going. Thank you for your intercession with men and with God.

Thank you also to Dr. James M. Renihan who not only taught me about theology and Baptist history, but who also helped me greatly with the bibliography by allowing me to find the most essential works for this dissertation. Thank you for the promptness of your responses to my numerous e-mails and questions, particularly while I was writing the introduction to this work. Thanks to Dr. Richard C. Barcellos who opened my understanding to John Owen's writings and who made many useful suggestions to improve this work. I would also like to thank other teachers who helped me to better understand Covenant and Baptist theology: Dr. Fred A. Malone, Dr. Samuel E. Waldron, Dr. Thomas J. Nettles. Thanks to Dr. Meine Veldman and Dr. Michael A.G. Haykin for their comments that helped reshape some areas of this dissertation. I want to take this opportunity to thank the *Faculté de Théologie Évangélique de Montréal* where I was trained in theology, especially to the dean, Dr. Amar Djaballah, one of the men of God who has greatly influenced my thought.

Thanks to Brother Guy Leroux for the design of the cover page. Thanks to Brother Steve Cyr who promptly agreed to replace me as chaplain at the prison. Thank you to all those who preached during my absence: Antoine Robillard, Réal Cyr and the pastors of the Association of Reformed Baptist Churches of Quebec. Thanks to

François Comeault who allowed me to benefit from his computer access to essential works of the seventeenth century to which I would not otherwise have had access. Thanks to his wife Linda Cyr who translated all English quotes for the publication of this work in French. Thanks to Mac Wigfield and his daughter Elizabeth for preparing the English version of this book.

Above all of these people, I give thanks to Him who alone is worthy of all glory, honour and praise; our God who gave his only Son to be the eternal mediator of a covenant as sure and permanent as his own life which is the guarantor. Lord, I have been overwhelmed and transformed while contemplating unveiled the glory of the Covenant of your grace. May all praise be yours!

I would like to dedicate this work to my beloved colleagues who are faithful ministers of Christ and with whom I proudly bear the name Reformed Baptist. I was speaking to you while writing these lines. I see you as champions of grace and truth. I would not want to serve our Master under any other covenant than the one that unites us and that we all cherish dearly.

Pascal Denault,
St-Jérôme, Qc
September 2012

Introduction

There is no doubt that the Baptists and paedobaptist Presbyterians of the seventeenth century were theologically close. The quasi-identical nature of the Westminster Confession of Faith and the Second Confession of Faith of London bear witness to this undeniable fact. In this work, we will, none the less, investigate not what united the Baptists and paedobaptists,[1] but rather what distinguished them.

1. HYPOTHESIS

The most obvious distinction between Baptists and Presbyterians is, of course, baptism. However, baptism is not the fundamental distinctive between these two groups. We propose that covenant theology is that distinctive between Baptists and paedobaptists and that all the divergences that exist between them, both theological and practical, including baptism, stem from their different ways of understanding the biblical covenants. Baptism is, therefore, not the point of origin but the outcome of the differences between paedobaptists and credobaptists. Ligon Duncan writes: "The biggest point of issue between the Baptist position on baptism and the Presbyterian or the paedobaptist position on baptism is not in our doctrine of the sacraments. It is in our doctrine of the church."[2]

---

[1] Unless otherwise specified, we will use the term Paedobaptist to identify the Christians of Presbyterian conviction in seventeenth-century England since it was mainly with them that the Baptists debated on the issues which we will develop in this dissertation. Similarly, we will use the word Baptist to specifically designate the English seventeenth-century Baptists, particularly the Calvinist Baptists associated with the Confession of Faith of 1689.

[2] Ligon Duncan, *Covenant Theology; The Abrahamic covenant – Covenant Sign Implications*, 12 two-hour lectures from the RTS Covenant Theology Course. Duncan's course, along with many other resources on covenant theology, is available from the following address:
http://www.fpcjackson.org/resources/apologetics/Covenant%20Theology%20&%20Justific ation/index.htm

It was not baptism in itself which was the point of dissent; but baptism as approached through the doctrine of the Church (which had no frame other than covenant theology). Before asking the question "Who can be baptized?" there was a more fundamental question, namely: "Who is in the covenant?" This is the most fundamental consideration in defining the Baptists' identity. To a point where, despite the great proximity between Congregationalist and Baptist ecclesiology, this question constituted the dividing point between the two groups instead of the point which drew them together. James Renihan writes: "This is not to say that their views were mutually exclusive, it is simply to say that ecclesiology was the driving force behind the Baptist movement, and provided it with a self-conscious identity distinct from that of the Independents."[3]

Baptists did not consider the question of baptism as a separate issue; for them, this question was intrinsically linked to their theology as a whole and to their overall understanding of the Scriptures. They rejected paedobaptism based on more than an analysis of the practice of baptism in the New Testament and the fact that no examples of child baptism are found there. This type of argument—regulatory principle, definition of baptism in the New Testament, etc.—was of secondary importance in Baptist apologetics. The debate surrounding baptism involved an issue much greater than that of a sacramental practice. It was a debate about the structure of the Scriptures; the meaning and the nature of the different covenants that God made with man; continuity and discontinuity in the revelation and carrying out of the plan of God; the very nature of the Gospel and of the Church was at the heart of this debate.[4] The Baptists were not only contesting a practice that

---

[3] James M. Renihan, *Edification and Beauty: The Practical Ecclesiology of the English Particular Baptists, 1675-1705*, Eugene, OR, Wipf & Stock, 2009, p. 37. Obviously, they were even more different from Presbyterians than from the Independents (i.e. Congregationalists).

[4] Later, Charles Spurgeon wrote: "The doctrine of the covenant lies at the root of all true theology. It has been said that he who well understands the distinction between the covenant of works and the covenant of grace, is a master of divinity. I am persuaded that most of the mistakes which men make concerning the doctrines of Scripture are based upon fundamental errors with regard to the covenants of law and grace." C.H. Spurgeon,

appeared misguided, but they took on a global theological system underlying this practice, thereby defying the very fundamentals of Presbyterian federalism.[5]

Baptists were therefore not looking to first define the doctrine of baptism in order to adjust to it the doctrine of the Church. Their doctrine of baptism was the outcome of a theological approach, similar in many ways, but at the same time clearly different from that of the majority of paedobaptists of their era. The question that preoccupied them was not simply to know who could be baptized so as to have a biblical practice of baptism. The issue that made them Baptists was to know who makes up the people of God. This query brought up a host of other questions that gave birth to a covenant theology different from the one inherited from the Reformation. Evidently, Baptists and paedobaptists did not have the same opinion on who makes up the Church. When they debated this question and its corollaries, baptism became the concrete manifestation of their respective convictions. According to David Benedict, the debate surrounding baptism which began in the mid seventeenth century, brought about an innovative approach to federal theology.[6] Theological contemplation was flourishing during this era and it had federal theology as its framework. Baptists were born in this context of theological progress; their sudden appearance is in itself a ramification of reformed thought. In the space of a few decades, Baptists articulated a theology all their own. The objective of our

---

"Sermon XL, The Covenant," *The Sermons of Rev. C.H. Spurgeon of London*, 9th Series, New York, Robert Carter & Brothers, 1883, p. 172.

[5] Federal theology (foedus = covenant) and covenant theology are synonymous expressions.

[6] David Benedict, *A General History of the Baptist Denomination in America and Other Parts of the World*, New York, Lewis Colby and Company, 1850, p. 146. Covenant theology began before the seventeenth century but the dialogue between Presbyterians and Baptists brought about great progress for federal theology. The paedobaptist covenant theology developed progressively from the beginning of the Reformation to its mature expression in the context of the Westminster Assembly. (Cf. Mark W. Karlberg, *Covenant Theology in Reformed Perspective*, Eugene OR, Wipf and Stock Publishers, 2000, p. 17-38.) But the federalism of Westminster was quickly put to the test with the coming of the Baptists. The paedobaptists were forced to fine tune their line of reasoning, even to the creating of new positions within the paedobaptist group.

work will be to bring to light the specific nature of this theology, particularly their distinct understanding of biblical covenants.

2. METHODOLOGY AND ORIGINAL SOURCES

One of the difficulties of our work comes from there having been no consensual interpretation of covenant theology either among paedobaptists[7] or Baptists. When we try to define the paedobaptist approach, we will be unable to present a definition encompassing all the pieces. Similarly, there are several discordant aspects on the Baptist side.[8] We will attempt, at the very least, to circumscribe the general theological principles characterizing the two parties which will be compared. Our method will consist in defining the fundamental difference between the seventeenth-century Presbyterians and Baptists based on their dialogue preserved through their writings. We will use the original sources directly. These sources are made up of confessions of faith and various treatises written by paedobaptist and Baptist theologians.[9]

---

[7] In "Works in the Mosaic Covenant: A Reformed Taxonomy", *The Law Is Not Of Faith: Essays on Works and Grace in the Mosaic Covenant*, Phillipsburg, P&R, 2009, p. 76-103, Brenton C. Ferry begins his chapter by a quote of Anthony Burgess, a seventeenth-century paedobaptist theologian, concerning covenant theology: "I do not find in any point of Divinity, learned men so confused and perplexed (being like Abraham's Ram, hung in a bush of briars and brambles by the dead) as here." His presentation quickly convinces that there was no uniformity among reformed covenantalists. Despite the many nuances we find among paedobaptist theologians of that era concerning covenant theology, we believe that there were common denominators that we will try to highlight in this present work.

[8] Moreover, they themselves admit it in the appendix to the Confession of Faith of 1689.

[9] Since the field of study of this work is covenant theology in seventeenth-century England, we will be unable to evaluate the current debate between Reformed Baptists and paedobaptists in a satisfactory way. Nevertheless, we hope to be able to show, here and there, the historical continuity between the seventeenth-century debate and the one taking place today by highlighting the great theological principles that have persisted through history and by occasionally intermixing the discussion between ancient and modern authors. Concerning the historical continuity of the reformed approach, we recommend the work of Richard C.

Although our work relates to historical theology, we will approach it from the angle of biblical and systematic theology. We will, therefore, not follow the development of the Baptist way of thinking in linear fashion, but will present this perspective by following the biblical order of the covenants. This method will allow us to further systemize Baptist theology in order to compare it with paedobaptist theology.

2.1. Confessions of faith and catechisms

Two documents are particularly germane to our research: the Westminster Confession of Faith and the Second London Confession of Faith, known as that of 1689. These documents are important since they do not represent the opinion of one isolated theologian, but the official positions adopted respectively by paedobaptists and Baptists. The Confession of 1689 is, in fact, a Baptist version of the Westminster Confession of Faith. It is, therefore, essential to see how the Baptists modified this Confession of faith: what they kept, what they omitted, reformulated or added.[10]

The First London Confession of Faith (1644-46) reveals itself equally as an important source. Although it does not present a covenant theology in substance, it allows us to ascertain that, from

---

Barcellos, *The Family Tree of Reformed Biblical Theology: Geerhardus Vos and John Owen, Their Methods of and Contributions to the Articulation of Redemptive History*, Owensboro, Reformed Baptist Academic Press, 2010, 324 pp. Barcellos demonstrates the close continuity between seventeenth-century covenant theology and twentieth-century biblical theology.

[10] Before being modified by the Baptists, the Westminster Confession was amended by the Congregationalists in the Declaration of Savoy (1658). Most of the changes introduced by the Declaration of Savoy were adopted by the Baptists. In a few cases, however, they prefer the formulation of the Westminster Confession of faith to that of the Declaration of Savoy. As concerning covenant theology, surprisingly, the Declaration of Savoy remained quite faithful to that of Westminster. It appears that the Congregationalists, at least in their declaration, considered their ecclesiology separately since they maintained the same covenant theology as the Presbyterians while rejecting their ecclesiology. This is why we are not comparing the Confession of 1689 with the Declaration of Savoy, but with the Westminster Confession of Faith.

their beginnings, the Baptists adhered to the reformed approach for understanding the Scriptures and salvation in a covenantal framework.[11] What is more, as we will see, already in 1644 the Baptists had a unique comprehension of the Covenant of Grace and of the New Covenant.

To the confessions of faith, it is necessary to add the catechisms: the Shorter and Larger catechisms of Westminster as well as the Baptist Catechism.[12] One other catechism is very important in the study of Baptist theology in the seventeenth century: the Orthodox Catechism written by Hercules Collins, pastor of *Old Gravel Lane* Baptist Church, and published in 1680. Pastor Collins followed Heidelberg's Catechism while writing his; the particularities in his are, therefore, very significant. James Renihan has written about it as follows:

> This leading Particular Baptist minister understood that the theology articulated by the Heidelberg divines was consonant with his own and with the broader movement of which he was a part. Collins' choice of the title An Orthodox Catechism, is worthy of note, for it is a double entendre. While it obviously refers to the true character of the doctrines it promotes, it also identifies the source of those doctrines, the so-called Protestant Orthodox divines of Europe. Collins was making an emphatic statement: just as they are Orthodox, so also are we.[13]

---

[11] The First London Confession presents redemption in terms that refer directly to the *Pactum Salutis* and *Historia salutis* theologies of the reformed scholasticism. See, in particular, paragraphs XI and XII.

[12] Several secondary sources comment and interpret the aforementioned confessions and catechisms. Two commentaries on these documents can, however, be considered as original sources: David Dickson's commentary on the Westminster Confession of Faith published in 1684, *Truth's Victory Over Error*, and Benjamin Beddome's commentary on the Baptist Catechism published in 1776, *A Scriptural Exposition of the Baptist Catechism*.

[13] James M. Renihan, *True Confessions: Baptist Documents in the Reformed Family*, Owensboro, Reformed Baptist Academic Press, 2004, p. 235. It is obvious that the Baptists were concerned with identifying themselves with the heritage of the Reformation. This explains the close relationship of their official documents to those of the other reformed movements. This desire for unity did not

2.2. Paedobaptist and Baptist theologians

Here are a few sources that cannot be ignored upon entering the seventeenth-century debate regarding covenant theology. This list is not exhaustive but representative; it does not contain all the documents that we consulted, and even less all those that exist, but is limited to those that were the most useful. We will present in order the paedobaptist sources followed by the Baptist sources going from the oldest to the most recent.

2.2.1. The Paedobaptists

William Ames (1576-1633) took refuge in the Netherlands in 1610 due to the hostile climate towards Puritans in England. He was a member of the Dordrecht Synod which condemned Arminianism, and later became the rector of the University of Franekeradeel. Under his tutelage were two students who would become important theologians in the development of reformed federalism: Johannes Cocceius and Gisbertus Voetius. Ames' federalism followed the continuity of the development of paedobaptist theology, the principal emphases of which can be found in his work: *Medulla theologiae* (*The Marrow of Theology*, 1629). This book was the main vector in spreading Ames' influence, especially in New

---

keep them from stating their distinct convictions within these same documents. Nevertheless, they always did it with irenic attitude. In the appendix of the Second London Confession, the Baptists affirm having published their confession in order to demonstrate their unity with other protestant Christians. They add: "And although we do differ from our brethren who are paedobaptists in the subject and administration of Baptism, and such other circumstances as have a necessary dependence on our observance of that ordinance, and do frequent our own assemblies for our mutual edification, and discharge of those duties, and services which we owe unto God, and His fear to each other: yet we would not be from hence misconstrued, as if the discharge of our own consciences herein, did anyway disoblige or alienate our affections, or conversation from any others that fear the Lord; but that we may and do as we have opportunity participate of the labors of those, whom God hath endued with abilities above ourselves, and qualified, and called to Ministry of the Word [...] ."

England.[14] His writings were also circulated in England, particularly among the Puritans. Near the end of his life, Ames was the pastor of a refugee church who sought a membership entirely composed of regenerated believers. As a result, it is not surprising that the Congregationalists and the Baptists were greatly inspired by his theology.[15]

John Ball (1585-1640) was a Presbyterian Puritan whose theology corresponds greatly to that of the Westminster Assembly. He died shortly before this major assembly was held, but his work, *A Treatise of the Covenant of Grace*, published in 1645, allowed him to have an effect on its outcome. The covenant theology presented by Ball represented the typical Presbyterian federalism which the Baptists took on. Ball was sometimes cited as an authority on reformed federalism by other Presbyterian authors. Available as a facsimile of the original edition, this source is considered as essential reading, especially since Ball criticized the separatist ecclesiology with which the Baptists have a lot in common.

Peter Bulkeley (1583-1659) was a Puritan theologian who was the rector of the Odell Parish in Bedfordshire.[16] He sided with the non-conformists before the First English Civil War and exiled himself in New-England to enjoy greater freedom. He wrote a treatise dedicated to covenant theology which was published in London in 1646: *The Gospel Covenant; or the Covenant of Grace Opened.*

Thomas Blake (1597-1657) was also a Puritan with Presbyterian convictions. Blake's treatises on covenant theology are important

---

[14] *The Marrow of Theology* was the basic instruction manual at Harvard during the time of the colonies and was long considered to be the best summary of Calvinist theology, cf. Joel Beeke &, Randall Pederson, *Meet the Puritans*, Grand Rapids, Reformation Heritage Books, 2006, p. 47ff.

[15] Thomas Goodwin, a congregationalist, believed that *The Marrow of Theology* was, after the Holy Scriptures, the best book in the world; *ibid.*, p. 45. The Baptists used this same work as a source when writing the First London Confession of faith in 1644, 46; cf. James M. Renihan, *True Confessions: Baptist Documents in the Reformed Family*, p. 3f.

[16] *Alumni Cantabrigienses,* Cambridge University Press. Available online at: http://venn.lib.cam.ac.uk/acad/search.html

since they start a dialogue with the opponents of child baptism, in particular with John Tombes.[17] We were unable to consult all of Blake's works, but the following was of great use in our research: *Vindiciae Foederis; or A Treatise of the Covenant of God Entered With Man-Kinde, In the Severa Kindes and Degrees of it*, published in London in 1653.

Herman Witsius (1636-1708), although he was a continental theologian, exacted a determining influence on federal theology in England. His federalism is, in some ways, the pivotal point between the federalism of continental theologians, including Zwingli, Bullinger, Calvin, Ursinus, Olevianus and Cocceius and that of the reformed in England.[18] His authoritative work, published in four volumes, *The Economy of the Covenants Between God and Man* (1677), is considered by many to be the definitive expression of reformed paedobaptist orthodoxy.

Samuel Petto (1642-1711) is the unknown figure in English theology.[19] Yet Petto was one of the strongest defenders of paedobaptism based on covenant theology and was an important questioner of the Baptists during the second half of the seventeenth century.[20] His most significant work is *The Great Mystery of the*

---

[17] John Tombes, despite a slight vacillation between Presbyterian and Baptist doctrine, opposed, both in writing and during public debates, the theology behind Paedobaptism. Cf. H. Leon McBeth, *The Baptist Heritage, Four Centuries of Baptist Witness*, Nashville, Broadman Press, 1987, p. 110f. Baptist historians do not generally consider Tombes as a Baptist but rather as an anti-paedobaptist.

[18] James Packer, in the introduction to the re-edition of *The Economy of the Covenants Between God and Man*, presents the work of Witsius as being the synthesis of Reformed covenant theology of his time. As we will see, the proximity between Witsius' theology and that related to the work of the Westminster Assembly is undeniable.

[19] This is how Mark Jones introduces Petto in comparison with John Owen, the forgotten figure of English theology. *The Great Mystery of the Covenant of Grace*, Stoke-on-Trent, Tentmaker Publications, 2007, p. 9. John Owen wrote the preface of this treatise and warmly recommended its reading.

[20] *Ibid.*, p. 10. In certain respects, Petto's theology is in line with the Baptists' as opposed to the traditional Presbyterian position. For example, Petto rejected the *one covenant two administrations* model as an explanation of the Covenant of Grace and its relation to the Old and New Covenants. Along with the Baptists, he considered that the Old and New Covenants were not two administrations of a

Covenant of Grace which was republished in 2007. This piece of writing is particularly important for the subject that we are studying since it takes into account the weaknesses of which the Baptists accused Presbyterian federal theology and tries to defend them. Another of his treatises is a direct response to a Baptist publication: *Infant-Baptism Vindicated from the Exceptions of Mr. Thomas Grantham*, published in 1691. A third work of Petto, *Infant Baptism of Christ's Appointment* broaches paedobaptism from the angle of covenant theology[21].

Francis Turretin (1623-1687) was not, of course, an English theologian. It is, however, interesting to notice the similarities between the Geneva Academy and the theology of Westminster during the seventeenth century. Turretin had an influence on the Puritans. His *Institutio Theologiae Elencticae* immediately represented the standard theology of the reformed school of thought. In it, Turretin's covenant theology is presented in the twelfth subject, entitled: *The Covenant of Grace and Its Twofold Economy in the Old and New Testaments.*[22] The title alone of this section of his work allows us to see that the Presbyterian model of the Covenant of Grace—one covenant under two administrations—was generalized.

2.2.2. The Baptists

John Spilsbury (1598-1668) belongs to the first generation of Calvinist Baptists and is the first pastor of the first Calvinist Baptist

---

single covenant but two distinct covenants. Petto is one of the Paedobaptsits who readjusted their federalism by adopting a median stance. We believe that the Baptist statement of position played a part in this.

[21] For a brief and efficient analysis of Petto's theology and in particular his distinct views of the Mosaic Covenant as a republication of the Covenant of Works, cf. Michael Brown, *Christ and the Condition: The Covenant Theology of Samuel Petto (1624-1711)*, Grand Rapids, Reformation Heritage Books, 2012, 139 pp.

[22] Francins Turretin, *Institutes of Elenctic Theology*, Phillipsburg, P&R, 1992, volume 2, p. 169.

church founded in 1638.[23] He is one of the signatories of the First London Confession of Faith of 1644 and of its revised version two years later.[24] One year before the issuing of this confession of faith, Spilsbury published a treatise on baptism entitled *A Treatise Concerning the Lawfull Subject of Baptisme*. In it he presents an understanding of covenant theology that is radically different from that of his contemporary paedobaptists. It is very significant that one of the oldest treatises of the Particular Baptists,[25] defending credobaptism, does so based on covenant theology. This shows that the Baptist identity held, from its beginning, a distinct federalism and that the baptism of believers was the result of a different understanding of the biblical covenants.[26]

Henry Lawrence (1600-1664) was a Puritan and a statesman closely associated with Oliver Cromwell. According to the biographical summary in the Encyclopedia Britannica: *Dictionary of National Biography*, Lawrence was dedicated to political and not ecclesiastical functions.[27] We do not know if Lawrence officially joined the ranks of the Baptists, but the treatise that he published anonymously, entitled *Of Baptism* (1646) leaves no doubt as to his theology. Lawrence adamantly criticized paedobaptist theology and defended a federalism coherent with credobaptism.

---

[23] The baptism of believers by aspersion was not, however, replaced by immersion until 1640.

[24] The two exact titles are respectively: *The Confession of Faith, of those Churches which are commonly (though falsly) called Anabaptists*, London, 1644. *A Confession of Faith, of the Severall Congregations or Churches of Christ in London, which are commonly (though unjustly) called Anabaptists*, The second Impression corrected and enlarged, London, Printed by Matth. Simmons, 1646.

[25] To our knowledge, two Particular Baptists defended credobaptism in writing before Spilsbury: Robert Barrow (1642) and Andrew Ritor (1642). Spilsbury seems nonetheless to be the first to have done it using covenant theology extensively.

[26] It is legitimate to wonder if the same thing can be said for the paedobaptists: was their practice of baptism a result of their covenant theology or was the opposite true? Otherwise put, did the paedobaptists develop their covenant theology in such a way as to justify paedobaptism?

[27] Gordon Goodwin, "Lawrence, Henry," *Dictionary of National Biography*, London, Smith, Elder & Co., 1892, volume 32, p. 256-58.

Thomas Patient (?-1666) was the pastoral assistant to William Kiffin in London. He was at the heart of the effervescent growth of the Baptist movement during the 40s and 50s[28] and was one of the signatories to the First London Confession of Faith. Sent as a missionary to Ireland by the Cromwell government, Patient established the first community of Baptist conviction there: *Waterford Baptist Church.*[29] During his time in Ireland, he wrote a treatise: *The Doctrine of Baptism, And the Distinction of the Covenants* (1654). In it, Patient clearly denounces paedobaptist theology as being an incorrect understanding of the biblical covenants while particularly attacking the Presbyterian paradigm: one covenant under two administrations.

John Bunyan (1628-1688) is certainly one, if not the best known, of the Puritans. He is often considered as being a part of Baptist tradition, although the church of which he was the pastor was not a Baptist church as such. Nevertheless, it is true that Bunyan's theology was very similar to that of the Baptists and the Congregationalists and that he was baptized into the Bedford Church by immersion. Bunyan's works are considerable in number and consist mainly of sermons. Bunyan also wrote a treatise on covenant theology which is found in the collection of his works published in three volumes by The Banner of Truth Trust entitled: *The Doctrine of the Law and Grace Unfolded.*

Edward Hutchinson was a Calvinist Baptist who defended credobaptism by opposing himself to Presbyterian federalism. We know very little about his life, only that he was the pastor of a Baptist congregation in Ireland.[30] He published an important treatise in 1676 in which he directly addressed the relationship between the

---

[28] Historians believe that the Particular Baptist movement officially began around 1638 and that by the end of the 50s, there were around 130 Calvinist Baptist churches in the British Isles. The singular context of the First English Revolution explains this astounding growth.

[29] Cf. Crawford Gribben, *The early Irish Baptists*, Escondido, The Institute of Reformed Baptist Studies, March 17, 2008, available at: http://www.reformedbaptistinstitute.org/?p=60

[30] Joseph Ivimey, *A History of the English Baptists*, London, Printed by Burditt and Morris, 1811, p. 404.

Covenant and baptism: *A Treatise Concerning the Covenant and Baptism.*[31] To this same treatise, he added two appendices: *Some Short Questions and Answers for the Yougner Sort,* as well as a response to a paedobaptist treatise: *Animadversions Upon a Late Book, Intituled, Infant Baptism From Heaven and not of Men, In Answer to Mr. Henry Danvers his Treatise of Baptism.*

Nehemiah Coxe (?-1688) is, in our humble opinion, the most significant Baptist theologian when it comes to covenant theology. He was the son of Benjamin Coxe, one of the signatories to the First London Confession of Faith.[32] His treatise, *A Discourse of the Covenants that God made with men before the Law* (1681)[33] outlines the fundamental differences between the Presbyterians and the Baptists based on their respective understanding of the Abrahamic Covenant. Coxe summarizes the Baptist distinction as follows: "the Old Covenant and the new differ in substance and not only in the manner of the administration."[34] The rest of his work is dedicated to showing the Old and New Covenants are not two administrations of one and the same covenant, but two distinct covenants.

Coxe's federalism is even more important since he was the principal artisan of the Second London Confession of Faith officially adopted by the Baptist churches of England in 1689.[35] In light of Coxe's treatise on covenant theology, the distinctive formulation of chapter 7 of the Second London Confession of Faith becomes particularly significant. Because of the pertinence of

---

[31] Thomas Delaune, Hutchinson's son-in-law, wrote a preface in this book; *ibidem.*

[32] Cf. James M. Renihan, "An Excellent and Judicious Divine: Nehemiah Coxe," *Covenant Theology: From Adam to Christ,* Palmdale, Reformed Baptist Academic Press, 2005, p. 7-11.

[33] The Reformed Baptist Academic Press publishing house released a modern edition of this book in 2005 paired with John Owen's exposition of Chapter 8 verses 6-13 of the Epistle to the Hebrews.

[34] Nehemiah Coxe, "A Discourse of the Covenants that God made with men before the Law," *Covenant Theology: From Adam to Christ,* Palmdale, Reformed Baptist Academic Press, 2005 (1681), p.

[35] James M. Renihan, *An Excellent and Judicious Divine: Nehemiah Coxe,* p. 18-20. Cf. also: Michael Haykin, *Rediscovering our English Baptist Heritage, Kiffin, Knollys and Keach,* Leeds, Reformation Today Trust, 1996, p. 68-69.

Coxe's treatise in interpreting the Baptist confession of faith, his federalism can practically be considered as the standard of Calvinist Baptists.

Thomas Grantham (?-1692) was the most outstanding theologian of the General Baptists. He entered into dialogue with Samuel Petto and set forth a very coherent critique of Presbyterian federalism. We only gained access to the treatise written by Graham near the end of his life: *Truth and Peace or the Last and most Friendly Debate Concerning Infant Baptism* (1689). Even though he was Arminian, his federalism is, in many regards, in accordance with that of Calvinist Baptists; in fact, he supports his argument with the same Coxe treatise.[36]

Benjamin Keach (1640-1704) is, without a doubt, the principal Baptist theologian of the second half of the seventeenth century. He was a very prolific author, but he brought no new developments to Covenant doctrine. Neither of Keach's treatises that directly address this subject is focused on the controversy surrounding baptism: *The Everlasting Covenant* (1693); *The Display of Glorious Grace: Or, The Covenant of Peace Opened, In Fourteen Sermons* (1689). The fundamental Baptist distinctions are none the less present in them.

2.3. John Owen the Baptist

An attentive reader will note that our list of 15 theologians who contributed to the debate on covenant theology in the seventeenth century is incomplete. The name of one of the most influential English theologians of all times is missing: John Owen (1616-1683). Owen merits special mention since his federalism is similar to that of the Baptists even though he remained a paedobaptist all of his life.[37] It is, therefore, necessary to justify the fact that we will use a paedobaptist theologian to defend a Baptist theology.

---

[36] Thomas Grantham, *Truth and Peace or the Last and most Friendly Debate Concerning Infant Baptism*, London, Printed for the Author, 1689, p. 6.
[37] Owen was, at first, of Presbyterian conviction, but then, after reading *The Keys of the Kingdom of Heaven* by John Cotton, he became a Congregationalist. Cf.

First, let us note that Owen's position on the Old Covenant was mediating. This is Sinclair Ferguson's conclusion.[38] Richard Barcellos explains what Ferguson means:

> [...] Ferguson's understanding of Owen's mediating position has to do with the nature and function of the Old Covenant and its relation to the Adamic Covenant of Works, the Covenant of Grace, and the New Covenant. Unlike others, Owen did not believe that the Old Covenant was a covenant of works in itself or simply an administration of the Covenant of Grace.[39]

During Owen's era, there was an antinomian tendency—represented particularly by the Socinians—who considered the Old Covenant as being the Covenant of Works. Opposing this tendency was that of the Presbyterians who considered the Old Covenant as being a covenant of grace. Owen thought of the Old Covenant as being neither the Covenant of Works nor the Covenant of Grace; this is why Ferguson says that Owen's position was mediating. From what we can tell, this mediating position was also endorsed by the Baptists, something we will see later. Owen rejected the model of a covenant of grace under two administrations. While other paedobaptists saw the Old Covenant as being different in circumstance[40], but identical in substance to the New Covenant, Owen considered that the Old Covenant was different from the New Covenant both in circumstance and in substance.

John Owen, "A Review of the True Nature of Schism," *The Works of John Owen,* vol. 13, Carlisle, The Banner of Truth Trust, 1967 (1657), p. 223-4.

[38] Sinclair Ferguson, *John Owen on the Christian Life,* Carlisle, The Banner of Truth Trust, 1987, p. 28

[39] Richard Barcellos "John Owen and New Covenant Theology," *Covenant Theology: From Adam to Christ*, Palmdale, Reformed Baptist Academic Press, 2005, p. 321.

[40] The word circumstance is often used as a synonym of the word administration: The Old Covenant is a circumstance (administration) of the Covenant of Grace, the New Covenant is another. Sometimes we also find the word accident being used to designate the external provisions of a covenant. We will use the words "administration" and "circumstance" as equivalents.

Another reason which allows us to believe that the Baptists shared John Owen's federalism lies in their own writings. For example, Edward Hutchinson, after having presented his understanding of the Abrahamic Covenant and its connection to the Covenant of Grace, uses Owen's writings extensively to prove that he says the same thing about the covenants as the highly reputed doctor. He then declares to his paedobaptist interlocutors:

> And if our opponents think Dr. O. injured (as they are apt to clamour to that purpose) for our improvement of his words to our advantage, he being for paedobaptism; we say, that they are at liberty to reconcile his words to his practice if they can, to do which they have need of a considerable stock (but they are seldome unfurnisht) of artifice, and distinction, to help at this dead lift. The Dr. treating about the nature of the Covenant and promises made to Abraham, (and perhaps forgetting Infant-Baptism) opens and expounds them with such spirituality and Orthodoxy, as leaves no room for Infant Baptism but excludes it beyond all possibility of reconciliation.[41]

As a result, the Baptists thought that Owen's theology was in perfect harmony with their own and considered as inconsequential the fact that the Prince of Puritans held to paedobaptism.[42] They

---

[41] Edward Hutchinson, *A Treatise Concerning the Covenant and Baptism*, London, Printed for Francis Smith, 1676, p. 34-35. Elsewhere, Hutchinson calls upon once again Owen: "This is indeed the grand Fabrick [covenant theology] whereby Infant-Baptism has been of late Years supported; which if we can demolish the Super structure must needs fall, as now ingeniously acknowledged. Nor need we employ any greater strength against it then what Dr Owen lends us [...] where he solidly confutes the plea from the Birth-privilege, to Christian Ordinances. And therefore to produce Dr. Owen against Mr. Whiston is a sufficient Confutation..." Cf. *Animadversions Upon a Late Book, Intituled, Infant Baptism From Heaven and not of Men, In Answer to Mr. Henry Danvers his Treatise of Baptism*, p. 41.

[42] During our reading of Owen's writings, we noticed a contradiction. In "Of Infant Baptism and Dipping" *The Works of John Owen*, vol. 16, Owen declares that the children of believers are in the Covenant. This conception contradicts what he wrote elsewhere, in particular in his commentary on the Epistle to the Hebrews, wherein he affirms that all who are in the Covenant of Grace are

even considered that Owen, without realizing it, was destroying Presbyterian federalism in his writing and they put the *onus probandi* on the paedobaptists, leaving it up to them to explain Owen's theology with his practice of baptism. For example Owen wrote:

> And herein lay the great mistake of the Jews of old, wherein they are followed by their posterity unto this day. They thought no more was needful to interest[43] them in the covenant of Abraham but that they were his seed according to the flesh; and they constantly pleaded the latter privilege as the ground and reason of the former. It is true; they were children of Abraham according to the flesh: but on that account they can have no other privilege than Abraham had in the flesh himself; and this was, as we have showed, that he should be set apart as a special channel, through whose loins God would derive the promised Seed into the world. In like manner were they separated to be a peculiar people, as his posterity, from amongst whom He should be so brought forth.
>
> That this separation and privilege was to cease when the end of it was accomplished and the Messiah exhibited, the very nature of the thing declares; for to what purpose should it be continued when that was fully effected whereunto I was designed? But they would extend this privilege, and mix it with the other,

---

regenerated. How can the children of believers be in the Covenant of Grace if they are not all regenerated (which Owen did not believe)? In our humble opinion, this contradiction can be explained by a progression in the Owen's thinking (he wrote this treatise while he was still a Presbyterian; his theology changed when he became a Congregationalist). We believe that his commentary on the Epistle to the Hebrews represents the mature and definitive thinking of Owen.

[43] The word "interest" has a very specific use in the writings of federal theology of the seventeenth century; consequently, it is used often. Here is the definition of the *Oxford English Dictionary*: "The relation of being objectively concerned in something, by having a right or title to, a claim upon, or a share in. [...] b. Right or title to spiritual privileges." Let us note Owen's passive use of the word: the Jews believed that their Abrahamic lineage conferred on them a right (interest) in the Covenant of Grace.

contending that, because they were the children of Abraham according to the flesh, the whole blessing and covenant of Abraham belonged unto them. But as our Saviour proved that in the latter sense they were not the children of Abraham, because they did not the works of Abraham; so our apostle plainly demonstrates, Rom. iv. ix. x. xi., Gal. iii. iv., that those of them who had not the faith of Abraham had no interest in his blessing and covenant. Seeing, therefore, that their other privilege was come to an end, with all the carnal ordinances that attended it, by the actual coming of the Messiah, whereunto they were subservient, if they did not, by faith in the promised seed, attain an interest in this of the spiritual blessing, it is evident that they could on no account be considered as actual sharers in the covenant of God.[44]

It would indeed seem that, in writing these lines and in thinking upon Covenant doctrine, Owen was not at all thinking about paedobaptism.

Another sign of the harmony between Owen's federalism and that of the Baptists comes from Nehemiah Coxe's introductory epistle in his book on covenants. Coxe explains to his readers why he stopped his exposition of the biblical covenants with the Abrahamic Covenant without going on to the Sinaitic Covenant. He writes:

Accordingly, I designed to give a further account of it in a discourse of the covenant made with Israel in the wilderness and the state of the church under the law. But when I had finished this and provided some materials also for what was to follow, I found my labor for the clearing and asserting of that point happily prevented by the coming out of Dr. Owen's third volume on Hebrews. There it is discussed at length and the objections that seem to lie against it are fully answered, especially in the exposition of the eighth chapter. I now refer my reader there for satisfaction about it which he will find

---

[44] John Owen, *Hebrews*, vol. 1, Carlisle, The Banner of Truth Trust, 1991, p. 122-123.

commensurate to what might be expected from so great and learned a person.[45]

We do not know if Owen endorsed Coxe's federalism. However evidently, Coxe, a Baptist, endorsed Owen's federalism. As we will see, Owen's commentary on chapter 8 of the Book of Hebrews leaves no doubt as to the consistency of his federalism with that of the credobaptists.

3. BRIEF HISTORICAL OVERVIEW OF COVENANT THEOLOGY

Covenant theology is a study of the different covenants that God has made with man since the beginning of the World. The connection between God and the creature of his making, as revealed in the Holy Scriptures, has always been defined in terms of covenants having different goals and terms. Since biblical history occurs entirely within these covenants, it is imperative to understand their nature and their role in order to correctly interpret the Scriptures. Consequently, covenant theology provides a context which allows for an understanding of the global structure of the plan of redemption by making the distinction between the parts and the whole and by explaining how these parts insert themselves into the whole.

This approach to Scripture is a fundamental characteristic of reformed theology.[46] It is in rediscovering justification by imputation that Zwingli, thanks to the parallel between Adam and Christ from Romans 5, also rediscovered the Adamic Covenant.[47] Then came the controversy with the Anabaptists which forced Zwingli to formulate his doctrine in terms that determined paedobaptist federalism in a definitive way. The insistence of the Anabaptists on the exclusivity of the New Testament to establish

---

[45] Nehemiah Coxe, *A Discourse of the Covenants that God made with men before the Law*, p. 30.
[46] Mark W. Karlberg, *Covenant Theology in Reformed Perspective*, p. 17.
[47] *Ibid.*, p. 20.

Church doctrine led Zwingli to defend the unity of the two testaments. For Zwingli, as for the reformed theologians who followed him, the substance of this unity resided in the Covenant of Grace. Thus, the reformed reading of the Scriptures consists first of all in a first covenant in Adam, eventually called the Covenant of Works. Then, immediately after the fall, God made a second covenant called the Covenant of Grace. The Covenant of Grace was placed under a first administration which we find in the Old Testament. This administration was elementary and temporary. Next came a second administration of the Covenant of Grace, which we find in the New Testament. This second administration is perfect and definitive.

The Reformed Church, therefore, saw the Old Covenant as a covenant of grace. This conception had a significant and definitive impact on reformed ecclesiology because, by considering that the Church was under the same covenant as Abraham's descendants, the Old Testament Scriptures became normative in defining the doctrine of the Church and its link to the Covenant of Grace. We find this predominant emphasis on the unity between the testaments in the works of practically all of Zwingli's successors.

Bullinger, in his treaty *De Testamento seu Foedere Dei Unico et Aeterno,* although he considered that the Old Covenant reaffirmed in its law the principle of the Covenant of Works, endorsed the idea that it was essentially an administration of the Covenant of Grace.[48] Just as other paedobaptist theologians who followed, Bullinger made a distinction between the substance and the circumstance of a covenant. The substance of the Old Covenant was the Covenant of Grace; its circumstance was the dispensation of the Old Testament.

No theologian had more influence on the reformed way of thinking than Calvin; his federalism is, therefore, important. Of course, the doctrine of the covenant underlies the whole of Calvin's thinking. However, chapters IX, X and XI of Book II of his

---

[48] *Cf. Ibid.,* p. 21-22.

Institutes of the Christian Religion specifically address this issue.[49] We find the main characteristics of paedobaptist federalism in Calvin's work. Just as his predecessors and his successors, he saw the Old and New Covenants as being two administrations of the Covenant of Grace: "The covenant made with all the fathers is so far from differing from ours in reality and substance, that it is altogether one and the same: still the administration differs."[50] He believes that the Covenant of Grace is a mixed covenant: "In this Church there is a very large mixture of hypocrites, who have nothing of Christ but the name and outward appearance[51]." And he justifies the baptism of believers' children on the basis of their belonging to the Covenant of Grace.[52]

Nevertheless, Calvin does not reject the apparent discontinuity between the Old and the New Covenant. In his commentary on Hebrews, he goes so far as to write: "The prophet might have otherwise said only, "I will renew the covenant which through your fault has come to nothing;" but he now expressly declares that it would be one unlike the former[53]." Calvin hereby states that the New Covenant is not simply a renewal of the Old Covenant, but, in fact, a New Covenant, or in other words, a different covenant. In spite of this, his other writings suggest that he saw the differences between the two covenants as being circumstantial in nature and not substantial.

---

[49] These chapters are respectively titled: (IX) Christ, though known to the Jews under the law, yet only manifested under the Gospel; (X) The resemblance between the Old Testament and the New; (XI) The difference between the two Testaments.

[50] *Institution*, II, X, 2. The formulation "one covenant two administrations" is not, however, as clear and frequent in Calvin's writings as it is with later reformed theologians. It seems that it is particularly with Ursinus that this notion becomes radical. Mark Karlberg writes: "Ursinus provides us here with a vital contribution in the development of the biblical interpretation of the covenant. With respect to the definition of covenant, Ursinus insists upon the importance of recognizing the substantial unity of the Covenant of Grace, but attempts at the same time to do fuller justice to the varying administrations of the divine covenant." *Covenant Theology in Reformed Perspective*, p. 26. Ursinus developed these notions in continuity with the thinking of his predecessors by bringing them further and developing them more clearly.

51 *Ibid.*, IV, I, 7.

52 *Ibid.*, IV, XVI, 5-6.

53 John Calvin, *Commentaries on the Epistle to the Hebrews*, Grand Rapids, Baker, 1999 (1549), p. 188.

In addition to underlining the discontinuity between the two covenants in his writings, Calvin draws another distinction that most of his successors did not. While commenting the third chapter of Paul's second Epistle to the Corinthians, Calvin indicates that the Covenant of Grace was not in itself a part of the substance of the Old Covenant:

> Both (Jeremiah and Paul), however, as they are contrasting the Old and New Testament, consider nothing in the Law but what is peculiar to it. For example, the Law here and there contains promises of mercy; but as these are adventitious to it, they do not enter into the account of the Law as considered only in its own nature[54].

It remains to be seen if Calvin understood the word Law, in this passage of Scripture, as referring to the Old Covenant. If this is the case, Calvin then makes a distinction that will be essential to Baptist theology: that the Covenant of Grace does not form part of the substance of the Old Covenant even if it was revealed during its administration. Unfortunately, Calvin does not further expand on this point. That would have required a reconsideration of the nature of the Old Covenant. We frequently encounter this type of tension in Calvin's theology, where what he states seems to be in opposition to what he said before[55]. Calvinism is a harmonization of doctrines that mutually complete each other. The successors of Zwingli, Bullinger and Calvin reaffirmed with greater clarity and precision what they themselves had already established.[56]

---

[54] John Calvin, *Institution*, II, XI, 7.
[55] Concerning this tension in Calvin's thought between the Covenant of Grace and the Covenant of Works in the Mosaic Covenant, cf. J. V. Fesko, " Calvin and Witsius on the Mosaic Covenant", *The Law Is Not Of Faith,* pp. 28-33.
[56] Cf. Mark Karlberg, *Covenant Theology in Reformed Perspective*, p. 25-30.

Chapter 1
The Covenant of Works

1. DESCRIPTION AND FUNCTION OF THE COVENANT OF WORKS

Before asking ourselves what the Covenant of Works is, we must consider if such a covenant exists. Certain reformed theologians reject the concept of the Covenant of Works as it was developed starting at the end of the 16th century.[1] The advocates of the Covenant of Works were aware that the expression "Covenant of Works" cannot be found anywhere in Scripture. Not being explicitly affirmed in Scripture, the Covenant of Works would necessarily have been contained therein. They tried to prove the existence of this covenant based on the New Testament parallel between Adam and Christ. For example, Anthony Burgess demonstrated that without a covenant of works, the attribution of Adam's sin to his posterity would have no meaning.[2] The Puritans considered that the presence of a promise and of a threat accompanying the commandment in Genesis 2.16-17 was an indication that this was not a simple law, but a covenant.[3]

---

[1] The more elaborated concept of the Covenant of Works was developed near the end of the 16th century. At the time, the expression *foedus naturae* was used, but eventually the name "Covenant of Works" became more commonly used, cf. Willem J. van Asselt, *The Federal Theology of Johannes Cocceius: (1603-1669)*, Boston, Brill, 2001, p. 325. Certain reformed theologians of the past and present day do not completely endorse the later elaboration of the Covenant of Works. We refer our readers to the work of Jean-Léon Longa J'Ekolonga who made this the subject of his Master's dissertation: *L'accomplissement des promesses protoévangéliques de l'alliance adamique dans l'œuvre messianico-eschatologique de Jésus-Christ* (The accomplishment of the protoevangelical promises of the Adamic covenant in the messianic-eschaltological work of Jesus Christ), Faculté de théologie évangélique de Montréal, 2010, 131 p.

[2] Anthony, *Vindicie Legis: or , A Vindication of the Morall Law and the Covenants*, London, 1643 p. 106.

[3] *Ibid.*, p. 120

The Covenant of Works had a simple way of functioning: if Adam had obeyed, he and his posterity after him would have retained life and would have been sealed in justice; but his disobedience marked the entrance of death into the world. The fall placed Adam and all of his posterity under condemnation. The Covenant of Works was conditional and provided no way to expiate the offence in case of disobedience. In reformed theology, the Covenant of Works is seen as the foundation for the "retributive" justice of God, whereby obedience begets blessing and disobedience brings malediction. It is the Covenant of Works that founded the principle "do this and you shall live" (Lev 18.5; Gal 3.12) as well as the principle "the wages of sin is death" (Rom 6.23; Heb 10.28). Under the Covenant of Works, eternal life cannot be given freely, it must be earned.[4] But now, because of sin, the Covenant of Works is ineffective in giving life; it can only bring death (Gal 3.21; Rom 8.3).

Reformed theologians considered that the Covenant of Works remained in effect after the fall,[5] but that the features inside this

---

[4] Peter Bulkeley makes a very pertinent remark regarding the revelation of the Covenant of Works versus the revelation of the Covenant of Grace: "The covenant of works is revealed by the light of Nature, but the covenant of grace is revealed by a supernatural light from above. Nature's light teaches men to look for life and righteousness by works, and this is written in all men's hearts, Rom. 2.15." *The Gospel Covenant; or The Covenant of Grace Opened*, London, Printed by M.S. for Benjamin Allen, 1646, p. 98. Bulkeley continues by explaining that it is natural for men to seek justification through works, grace being contrary to natural reasoning.

[5] Arminius rejected the idea that the Covenant of Works remained in effect after the fall, because, according to him, God cannot require of man something that he is unable to do. To demand perfect obedience from a fallen creature would have been unjust. Cf. Herman Witsius, *The Economy of the Covenants Between God and Man*, Kingsburg CA, den Dulk Christian Foundation, 1990, vol. 1, p. 151ss. The Calvinists did not consider it unjust to require such obedience from a creature incapable of this obedience, since this requirement was given while man was still able to comply. Man changed, but the divine standards of justice remain the same. The Covenant of Works allowed the Calvinists to say that God could have unilaterally condemned all men while remaining just, even if none of them could have obeyed.

covenant changed after the entry of sin into the world. Before the fall, man benefited from a relationship with his Creator wherein, by virtue of the Covenant of Works, God was his God. While remaining under the obligation of obeying God because of this covenant, fallen man lost his covenantal privileges which ensured him of God's favour and found himself, from then on, under God's wrath. While God remained God for all men even after the fall, sin made it so that He was no longer their God in a favourable covenantal connection. John Owen summarizes the Puritan conception of the Covenant of Works after the fall as follows: "And man continued under an obligation to dependence on God and subjection to his will in all things. [...] But that especial relation of mutual interest by virtue of the first covenant ceased between them."[6]

The writings of the Baptists show that they shared this same conception of the Covenant of Works as their paedobaptist contemporaries. It is, however, remarkable to note that the Confession of 1689 removed almost all mention of the Covenant of Works that was to be found in the Westminster and Savoy confessions.[7] The only place where the Covenant of Works is directly referenced in the Confession of 1689 is in chapter 20, paragraph 1.[8] There is no doubt that the Baptist Confession of faith endorses the doctrine of the Covenant of Works, but it is presented differently. What is more, certain formulations that can be found in these sister confessions of faith were rejected to avoid ambiguous wording.[9] Thus, it is terminological reasons, not theological reasons

---

[6] John Owen, "An Exposition of Hebrews 8:6-13: Wherein, the nature and differences between the Old and New Covenants is discovered," *Covenant Theology: From Adam to Christ*, Palmdale, Reformed Baptist Academic Press, 2005, p. 281.

[7] Here are the paragraphs of the Confession of 1689 where the references to the Covenant of Works were removed. 6.1; 7.2; 19.1; those that make reference to the Covenant of Works without naming it: 4.3; 7.2; 19.1, 2; and those where the expression "Covenant of Works" can be found: 19.6 (2x); 20.1.

[8] "Covenant of Works" is used twice in 19.6; however, it does not refer to the Covenant of Works made with Adam, but rather to the concept of such a covenant.

[9] For a more complete discussion of this topic and the ambiguities in question cf. Samuel Waldron, *A Modern Exposition of the 1689 Baptist Confession of Faith*,

that explain the way the Baptists treated the Covenant of Works in their confession of faith.

If Presbyterian and Baptist federalisms agree on the origin, the nature and the function of the Covenant of Works, we, however, note a divergence of views regarding the relationship between this covenant and the Old Covenant.

2. THE RELATIONSHIP BETWEEN THE COVENANT OF WORKS AND THE OLD COVENANT

The New Testament presents a contrast, or even an antithesis, between the law and grace (Rom. 6.14; Gal. 2.21, 3.18, 5.4). What does the word law refer to in these passages? Since the paedobaptists saw the Old Covenant as an administration of the Covenant of Grace in harmony with the New Covenant, according to them the opposition between the law and grace did not mean an opposition between the Old and the New Covenants, but rather an opposition between the Covenant of Works and the Covenant of Grace. Therefore, the law to which the Apostle Paul refers, when he opposes it to the Gospel, would be the Covenant of Works. This understanding in no way affects the definition of the Covenant of Works, but determines the definition of the Old Covenant and its rapport with the New Covenant.

Most of the paedobaptist theologians of the seventeenth century understood that "not to be under the law, but under grace" (Rom. 6.14), simply meant not to be under the Covenant of Works, but under the Covenant of Grace. For example, Herman Witsius explains that to be "under the curse of the law" (Gal. 3.10) does not mean to be under the Old Covenant, but under the Covenant of Works: "But many things prove that nothing is meant by the curse, but the curse of the Covenant of Works."[10] When the New Testament clearly

---

Webster, Evangelical Press, 1989, p. 94-96. In his course, *Baptist Symbolics*, James Renihan explains that the focal point of chapter 7 of the Baptist Confession of Faith is not exactly covenant theology, but rather the salvation of the elect. This chapter was edited so that all of the emphasis was put on the plan of salvation.
[10] Herman Witsius, *The Economy of the Covenants*, vol. 2, p. 359.

opposes the Old Covenant and the New Covenant (2 Cor. 3), Witsius indicates that it is a contrast of degrees inside the same Covenant of Grace and not a contrast between the Covenant of Works and the Covenant of Grace:

> I answer: the apostle does not here oppose the Covenant of Grace, as it is dispensed after the coming of Christ, to the same Covenant of Grace, as it was dispensed before, but opposes the Covenant of Grace, as in its full efficacy under the New Testament, to the national covenant made with the Israelites at Mount Sinai; and as a spiritual covenant to a typical.[11]

Witsius was not alone in relativizing the contrast Old/New Covenants to make absolute the Covenant of Works/Covenant of Grace contrast. According to Johannes Cocceius[12] and Robert Rollock,[13] the law under which Christ was born and the law which he fulfilled was strictly the Covenant of Works. Thomas Boston, uses rather the dualism of the two Adams which we find in 1st Corinthians 15: the first, Adam himself, and the second, Christ. Boston applies this terminology to the covenants: the first covenant, the Covenant of Works, and the second, the Covenant of Grace.[14] Boston's terminology corresponds to that of the Westminster and Savoy confessions who call the Covenant of Works "the first covenant" and the Covenant of Grace "the second covenant."[15] The understanding of the paedobaptists did not consider the Old and New Covenants as being antithetical, but isolated only the antithesis between the Covenant of Works and the Covenant of Grace. John Ball represents this

---

[11] *Ibid.*, p. 336

[12] J. van Asselt, *The Federal Theology of Johannes Cocceius,* p. 253.

[13] Robert Rollock, *A Treatise of our Effectual Calling,* Harvard College Library, 1828 (1597), p. 52

[14] Thomas Boston, *A View of the Covenant of Grace From the Sacred Records,* Glasgow, Printed by Robert and Thomas Duncan, 1770 (1742), p. 26ff.

[15] Cf. Chapter 7, paragraphs 2 and 4 of these confessions. This terminology is even more ambiguous than the New Testament making a comparison between a first and second covenant, not to designate the Covenant of Works and the Covenant of Grace, but in comparing the Old and New Covenants (cf. Heb. 8-9).

understanding exactly when he writes: "Some make the Old and New Testament, as the Covenant of works and grace, opposite in substance and kind, and not in degree alone: and that to introduce an unfound distinction."[16]

The Baptists accepted with no problem that the word law, used as an antithesis to the word grace, would refer to the Covenant of Works. Paragraph 2 of Chapter 7 of the 1689 reads: "Moreover, man having brought himself under the curse of the law by his fall [...]". The Baptists, however, refused to deny the continuity between the Covenant of Works and the Old Covenant. For them, the law/grace antithesis reflected the Old/New Covenant antithesis. This understanding is obvious in this quote from Benjamin Keach:

> Though evident it is that God afterwards more clearly and formally repeated this Law of Works to the People of Israel [...] though not given in that Ministration of it for Life, as before it was to Adam; yet as so given, it is by St. Paul frequently called the Old Covenant, and the Covenant of Works, which required perfect Obedience of all that were under it.[17]

Keach and the other Baptists believed that the Covenant of Works was reaffirmed in the Old Covenant, but for different reasons than when it was initially given to Adam. Contrarily to the Presbyterians, the Baptists understood the New Testament law/grace contrast as a contrast between the Old and New Covenants. For the paedobaptists, the expression "the curse of the law" referred directly to the Covenant of Works, while for the Baptists, it referred to the Covenant of Works, but as being reaffirmed in the Old Covenant. Therefore, in order to maintain unity and continuity between the Old and New Covenants,[18] the paedobaptists had to reject the unity and

---

[16] John Ball, *A Treatise of the Covenant of Grace*, Dingwall, Peter and Rachel Reynolds, 2006 (1645), p. 93.

[17] Benjamin Keach, *The Display of Glorious Grace: Or, The Covenant of Peace Opened. In Fourteen Sermons*, London, Printed by S. Bridge, 1698, p. 15.

[18] We consider that our readers understand why unity between the Testaments is fundamental to paedobaptism.

continuity between the Covenant of Works and the Old Covenant. Regarding the Covenant of Works, the difference between the tenants of the Westminster and those of the 1689 were found in their vision of the relationship between the Covenant of Works and the Old Covenant and, implicitly, from the link between the latter and the New Covenant. We will further develop this point when we specifically address the nature of the Old Covenant.

Chapter 2
The Covenant of Grace

In this chapter we will start by explaining the covenant of grace idea in the seventeenth century and continue by presenting two different understandings of the same covenant. The Covenant of Grace was the basis of federalism; this same basis became the breaking point between Presbyterian and Baptist theology. These two groups had a different understanding of the Abrahamic and Mosaic Covenants, and of the New Covenant, because they understood the Covenant of Grace differently. We will first examine their respective starting points to later observe their hermeneutic and theological distancing. We think that it is precisely here, meaning the notion of the Covenant of Grace, that everything is at issue between Presbyterianism and the Baptist movement.

1. THE COVENANT OF GRACE IN THE SEVENTEENTH CENTURY

With the rediscovery of salvation by grace during the reformation, the notion of a covenant of grace was developed. In the seventeenth century, federal theology was the frame within which all doctrines were understood and the doctrine of salvation by grace did not escape this frame. At that time, the topic of salvation by grace was not broached outside of the Covenant of Grace. While the two doctrines were not confused, neither were they separated. The Covenant of Grace, in reformed perspective, is the covenant that regroups all of the saved of all time from the creation of the world until the last judgement. All those who were objects of God's grace were in the Covenant of Grace.

Even if the revelation of grace was more apparent in the New Testament, no reformed theologians believed that salvation by grace started with the New Testament. From Luther, it was believed that the Gospel started being revealed as of Genesis 3 verse 15 and that the rest of the plan for redemption was progressively revealed starting with this promise that is often called proto-gospel. Reformed orthodoxy recognized only one Covenant of Grace within which only one Gospel and one redeemed people were found. There was, however, a theological approach rejecting the Covenant of Grace and inter-testamentary unity notions which came from this: the Socinian approach.

1.1. Socianism and the Covenant of Grace

The Socinians were among the main adversaries of reformed theology. Their understanding of the way the Old and New Testaments related to one another made them the "hyper-dispensationalists" of their time. For example, in their catechism, they defended a strict discontinuity between the two testaments: "Nowhere will you discover in the law of Moses, either eternal life or the gift of the Spirit promised to those obeying the precepts of the law, as it is evident they are promised in the law given by Christ."[1] David Dickson, in his exposition of chapter 7 of the Westminster Confession, highlighted the unity between the sacrifices of the Old Testament and the New Testament sacrifice and denounced the Socinians who denied this unity.

> Question I. *Did all these Sacrifices and other Types, and Ordinances by which the Covenant of Grace was administered before our Saviours Incarnation, adumbrate, and foresignify Christ to come?*
> Yes. Heb: 8, 9, 10, chapters; Rom: 4.11. Col: 2.11, 12. 1 Cor: 5.7
> Well then, do not the Socinians err, who maintain, *that the Legal Sacrifices did not foresignify the expiatory Sacrifice of Christ, neither were types nor Figures of it; by that those Sacrifices, which the Jews Offered for sin, did really and in very deed, purge away all the sins for which they were offered?*
> Yes.

---

[1] *Racovian Catechism* 5, 1652, p. 133; quoted by Francis Turretin, *Institutes of Elenctic Theology*, Phillipsburg, P&R, 1992 (1696), vol. 2, p. 192.

By what reasons are they confuted? [...] [2]

Socinus himself confirms in his correspondence that Dickson presents the Socinian understanding in a fair way: "In this I disagree with you, that you seem to concede, that the pious under the Old Testament, looked to Christ in those ceremonies and sacrifices in which he was typified, and were saved in the hope of his coming, a thing of which I can in no way persuade myself."[3] Herman Witsius, for his part, described the Socinian position as "heretical": "[...] the heresy of the Socinians, who assert, with the utmost effrontery, that there was no promise of eternal life in the Old Testament; that Jesus Christ was the first and only preacher of that important truth."[4] As for John Owen, he compared Socianism to Pelagianism:

> Some indeed, in these latter days, have revived the old Pelagian imagination, that before the law men were saved by the conduct of natural light and reason; and under the law by the directive doctrines, precepts, and sacrifices of it, without any respect to the Lord Christ or his mediation in another covenant.[5]

In response to the Socinian dichotomy, the reformed put a predominant emphasis on the unity and continuity of the Covenant of Grace from the proto-gospel to its full accomplishment in the death and resurrection of Christ. This is how the main biblical covenants were unified and how the notion of discontinuity in the divine plan was largely discarded. The Abrahamic, Sinaitic and Davidic Covenants were seen only as different administrations of the Covenant of Grace revealed to Adam and Eve in Genesis 3.15. The reformed considered that these covenants and the New Covenant were of the same substance, that is, grace, and that the

[2] David Dickson, *Truth's Victory Over Error*, Edinburgh, Printed by John Reid, 1684, Chap. VII. Of Gods Covenant With Man.
[3] Socinus, "Ad amicos epistolae: ad Matthaeum Radecium," *Opera Omnia*, 1656, vol. 1, p. 377, quoted par Francis Turretin, *Institutes of Elenctic Theology*, vol. 2, p. 192f.
[4] Herman Witsius, *The Economy of the Covenants*, vol. 2, p. 324.
[5] John Owen, *An Exposition of Hebrews 8:6-13*, p. 180.

disparate elements among these various covenants were only external and administrative factors. As soon as an author or a group questioned the organic uniformity of the Covenant of Grace, he was categorized with the Socinians, the Anabaptists and the Arminians. The first were antitrinitarian heretics, the second were reminiscent of Münster's fanaticism and the third were the adversaries of the theology of grace. These three groups also had in common their rejection of the inter-testamentary unity of the Covenant of Grace.[6]

It would be difficult to exaggerate the size of the challenge that the Baptists were up against: contesting the majority understanding of the Covenant of Grace by insisting on the discontinuity between the biblical covenants, while disassociating themselves from the Socinians, the Anabaptists and the Arminians. Disassociation from them was made even more difficult by the fact the Anabaptists and Socinians also rejected child baptism and only baptized believers. It is, therefore, not surprising that the Baptists were called Anabaptists and that they were marginalized, persecuted and that very few of the paedobaptists gave honest consideration to any of their arguments. From the beginning, the Baptists were caricatured and suspected of incarnating all of the theological and moral deviances of the past.[7] Their theology was, therefore, defined with precaution, particularly when they presented a different point of view. Regarding the

---

[6] Cf. Francis Turretin, *Institutes of Elenctic Theology*, vol. 2, p. 192-193. These groups could not conceive that faith in Christ could have existed under the Old Testament and found such a belief to be ridiculous and anachronistic. As an answer, Turretin demonstrates that the faith of the patriarchs was not only a faith that a Christ would come, but faith in Christ who would come (Ac 19.4-5).

[7] The title of the first confession of faith is very revealing: *"The Confession of Faith, of those Churches which are commonly (though falsly) called Anabaptists."* One of the goals of the publication of this first confession of faith was to dispel all suspicions surrounding their orthodoxy and practices. Daniel Featley, one of the instigators of these suspicions, recognized that the first edition of the Baptist Confession of Faith (1644) was orthodox, but he indicated in his reply (*The Dippers dipt. Or, The Anabaptists duck'd and plunged Over Head and Eares*, 1645) that the Baptists draped themselves in orthodoxy in order to hide their true nature and to avoid being sanctioned by the authorities. This information comes from James Renihan's course *Baptist Symbolics*.

Covenant of Grace, the Baptist position was in some ways midway between the strict continuity of the Presbyterian position and the radical discontinuity of the Socinians. In agreement with the Presbyterians against the Socinians, the Baptists affirmed the unity of substance of the Covenant of Grace from Genesis to Revelation. However, just like the Socinians, against the Presbyterians, they affirmed the discontinuity of substance between the Old and the New Covenants.

In the rest of this chapter, we will compare the Presbyterian and Baptist understandings of the Covenant of Grace. We will successively present both notions and then draw a few conclusions from our comparison.

2. THE COVENANT OF GRACE AS SEEN BY THE PAEDOBAPTISTS: ONE COVENANT UNDER TWO ADMINISTRATIONS

We have already mentioned several times, the Presbyterian paradigm of the Covenant of Grace which consists in seeing only one covenant administered respectively by the Old and New Covenants. This notion was definitively rooted in Presbyterian theology when it was integrated into the standards of Westminster: "This covenant [the Covenant of Grace] was differently administered in the time of the law and in the time of the gospel [...] "[8]

2.1. A fundamental distinction between the substance and the administration

The paedobaptists were not ignorant of the differences between the two testaments, but this is how they took them into consideration in their efforts to maintain the unity of the Covenant of Grace from the beginning to the end of the revelation. In examining the Covenant of Grace, two aspects of it had to be brought out: its substance and its circumstance or administration. This explanation is found in the opus magnum of Herman Witsius published in 1677:

---

[8] *The Westminster Confession of Faith*, VII, V.

It is a matter of the greatest moment, that we learn distinctly to consider the Covenant of Grace, either as it is in its *substance* or essence, as they call it, or as it is in divers ways proposed by God, with respect to *circumstantials*, under different economies. If we view *the substance* of the covenant, it is but only one, nor is it possible it should be otherwise. [...] But if we attend to the circumstances of the covenant, it was dispensed *at sundry times and in divers manners*, under various economies, for the manifestation of the manifold wisdom of God.[9]

This distinction was essential to Presbyterian federalism since it allowed for maintaining the unity of the Covenant of Grace while recognizing elements of discontinuity between its different administrations. Caspar Olevianus also applied this distinction to the Covenant of Grace. Lyle Bierma underlines how fundamental this was to his theology:

The key to Olevianus's doctrine of the Covenant of Grace is to be found in three distinctions he frequently makes: 1) an explicit distinction between the *substantia* and the *administratio* of the covenant; 2) a further, though implicit distinction between the outward *administratio* of the covenant promise to all within the visible Church and the inward *administratio* of the *substantia* of this promise to the elect; and 3) an implicit distinction between the covenant as a divine testament or promise, on the one hand and as a mutual binding of wills, on the other.[10]

Not only did the distinction between the substance and circumstance allow the Presbyterians to affirm the unity of the Covenant of Grace without denying the divergences between the testaments, but it also allowed them to justify the mixed nature of the people of God (made up of both regenerate and the non-regenerate) within the Covenant of Grace; which is even more fundamental to paedobaptism. By distinguishing the substance from

[9] Herman Witsius, *The Economy of the Covenants*, vol. 1, p. 291.
[10] Lyle Bierma, *The Covenant Theology of Caspar Olevianus*, Grand Rapids, Reformation Heritage books, 2005, p. 104-5.

the administration, the paedobaptists could consider a place for the non-chosen within the Covenant of Grace and thereby make a place for the natural posterity of believers. The external administration of the Covenant of Grace would, therefore, contain the regenerate and the non-regenerate, while its internal substance would only contain the regenerate. This is how, by distinguishing between the internal substance and the external administration, the paedobaptists justified the mixed nature of the Covenant of Grace. According to them, the non- regenerate of the Covenant of Grace benefited from a status among the people of God by being exposed to the preaching of the Gospel and in taking part in the sacraments. However, only the regenerate reaped the full benefits of the substance of the Covenant of Grace by virtue of the internal efficacy of the Holy Spirit. Hence, there was a natural way and a spiritual way to find oneself in the same Covenant of Grace.

Bierma affirms that the distinction between the substance and the administration lead directly to the mixed nature of the Covenant of Grace by introducing into it the unsaved.

> The first two of these [the first two distinctions mentioned in the last quote] are particularly helpful in solving some of the problems we encountered in the older research on Olevianus's covenant theology. For example, the relationship of the non-elect in the visible Church to the covenant is actually very clear [...] they are included in the external administration of the covenant through the Word and sacraments but not in the internal administration of the substance of benefits of the covenant through the Holy Spirit.[11]

By separating the substance from the administration and by making a distinction between an external (natural) efficacy and an internal (spiritual) efficacy of the Covenant of Grace, the paedobaptists justified the mixed nature of the biblical covenants. This notion was palpable in paedobaptist ecclesiology; it manifested

---

[11] *Ibid.*, p. 105.

itself in the concept of the visible and invisible Church.[12] For example, in Chapter 25 of the Confession of Westminster, these distinctions (substance/administration; internal/external; spiritual/ natural) are applied to the Church through the notion of visible and invisible Church:

> I. The catholic or universal Church, which is invisible, consists of the whole number of the elect, that have been, are, or shall be gathered into one, under Christ the Head thereof; and is the spouse, the body, the fullness of Him that filleth all in all.
>
> II. The visible Church, which is also catholic or universal under the Gospel (not confined to one nation, as before under the law), consists of all those throughout the world that profess the true religion; and of their children: and is the kingdom of the Lord Jesus Christ, the house and family of God, out of which there is no ordinary possibility of salvation.

Paragraph I, under the designation of invisible Church, presents the internal administration of the Covenant of Grace where only the chosen who have been called participate in the substance of this covenant. Paragraph II, under the designation of visible Church, indicates that all of those who profess, regenerated or not, including their posterity, form the Kingdom of Christ under the external administration of the Covenant of Grace. Here is how William Ames used the internal/external (substance/administration) distinction to justify the presence of non-regenerated "Christians" in the institution of the visible Church: "Those who are only believers by profession, while they remain in that society [the visible Church], are members of that church, as they are of the catholic church, so far

---

[12] Edward Hutchinson faulted the paedobaptists for using this concept in an equivocal way: "I answer; you delude us very often with the word (Visible) for sometimes your Infants are, sometimes they are not in the Covenant (visibly) so that this term is as ambiguous and mystical as words of *Cabal*." *A Treatise Concerning the Covenant and Baptism*, London, Printed for Francis Smith, 1676, p. 28-29.

as outward status is concerned. In inward or essential status, they do not belong."[13] The normal Church, for the paedobaptists, included, as part of the institution, professing people who were both regenerated and non-regenerated as well as the natural descendants of these people.

The paradigm *one covenant two administrations* of paedobaptist covenant theology involved two elements necessary to Presbyterian federalism: the unity of the Covenant of Grace from Genesis to Revelation and the mixed nature of the Covenant of Grace from Israel until the New Testament Church. This theoretical model was largely endorsed by seventeenth-century paedobaptists.

In the very formulation "one covenant under two administrations," we find the *substance/circumstance* distinction or even the *internal/external* or *spiritual/natural* or *invisible/visible* distinction. First, there is *one covenant* (internal spiritual and invisible substance) *under two administrations* (external natural and visible circumstance). This distinction is implicit in all of Presbyterian federalism and it is fundamental to it. For example, William Ames, in discussing the differences between the Old and New Covenants, uses this distinction which allows him to affirm the unity of substance and the discontinuity of administration between these two covenants: "The [new] testament is new in relation to what existed from the time of Moses and in relation to the promise made to the fathers. But it is new not in essence but in form." [14]

In distinguishing between the form and the essence (substance/administration), Ames confines the newness of the New Covenant to its external form, its substance being new in nothing. Consequently, for Ames and his paedobaptist contemporaries, there is identity of substance between the Old and New Covenants.[15] On

---

[13] William Ames, *The Marrow of Theology*, Grand Rapids, Baker, 1997 (1629), p. 179.

[14] *Ibid.,* p. 206.

[15] Presbyterian federalism was definitively characterized by the identity between the Old and New Covenants. Jeffrey Johnson, in *The Fatal Flaw of the Theology Behind Infant Baptism*, Free Grace Press, 2010, demonstrates, in chapter 3, that the notion of continuity of essence between the Old and New Covenants was taught by the principal paedobaptist theologians from the Reformation until the

the basis of this continuity, the paedobaptists established their principle of posterity by which the natural descendents of believers are integrated into the Covenant of Grace.

2.2. From the "one covenant under two administrations" model to the principle of succession

The identity of substance between the Old and New Covenants constituted the theological foundation of paedobaptism; Richard Pratt explains:

> When reformed theology speaks of baptism as covenantal, the sacrament is viewed in the context of the unity of the Covenant of Grace. The meaning of baptism is not found in the teachings of the NT alone; it is also inferred from the manner in which baptism fulfills OT patterns of faith. This reliance on the covenantal unity of both the OT and NT is stated in general terms when the Westminster Confession identifies the ordinances administered.[16]

The organic unity of the Covenant of Grace was, and remains, the cornerstone of paedobaptist theology. Under the Old Covenant, natural descendants were included in the covenant: "I will establish my covenant as an everlasting covenant between me and you and your descendants after you for the generations to come, to be your God and the God of your descendants after you." (Gen.17.7). If the New Covenant is substantially identical to the Old one, this principle of posterity must continue.

---

present day: Uldrich Zwingli, Henry Bullinger, John Calvin, Caspar Olevianus, Zacharia Ursinus, Thomas Cartwright, John Preston, Thomas Blake, John Ball, William Ames, Johannes Cocceius, Johannes Wollebius, Herman Witsius, Charles Hodge, James Buchanan, Robert Dabney, John Murray, Edward Young, James Bannerman, Meredith Kline, O. Palmer Robertson, Robert Reymond; this list is not exhaustive, but it is certainly representative.

[16] Richard L. Pratt Jr., "Reformed View: Baptism as a Sacrament of the Covenant," *Understanding Four Views on Baptism*, Grand Rapids, Zondervan, 2007, p. 65.

The Baptists did not deny the principle of natural posterity under the Old Covenant. However, they considered the importation of this principle under the New Covenant to be a fallacy dependant on an artificial and arbitrary construction of the Covenant of Grace.[17] They

---

[17] They also believed the paedobaptists did not apply this principle in a manner which was coherent with the way in which it was applied under the Abrahamic covenant. Nehemiah Coxe summarized his view thus: "They [the paedobaptists] generally narrow the terms of covenant interest [...] by limiting it to the immediate offspring. Yet in this covenant [the Abrahamic covenant] it was not restrained like this but came just as fully on remote generations. They also exclude the servants and slaves of Christians, with the children born of them, from that privilege which they suppose they enjoyed under the Old Testament in being sealed with the sign or token of the covenant of grace." *A Discourse of the Covenants*, p. 106.
Edward Hutchinson held the same position: "I challenge any man to give me a substantial ground, why the faith of a believer may not now as well inright [give right to] his children's children to the 3^d & 4th generation to Church-membership and Baptism, as the faith of *Abraham* did inright his seed in their generations to the priviledges of the old Covenant." *A Treatise Concerning the Covenant and Baptism*, p. 50. John Ball had no doubt noted this weakness in Presbyterian theology; he therefore explained that when a person abandoned the Covenant of the promise, all of his posterity lost the privilege of the covenant along with him. Rather than extend the New Covenant to the distant posterity of believers, Ball restrained the Old Covenant to the immediate posterity of believers. Cf. *A Treatise of the Covenant of Grace*, p. 202. Thomas Goodwin had a similar understanding: "A Discourse of Election" *The Works of Thomas Goodwin*, Volume 9, Grand Rapids, Reformation Heritage Books, 2006 (1682), p. 428. Naturally, the Baptist theologians believed that this way of proceeding was an artificial construction of the reach of the Old Covenant. Coxe wrote: "[T]he promises now given to Abraham [...] run to him and to his seed after him in their generations. The covenant itself is said to be an everlasting covenant which they are strictly commanded to keep in their generations (Genesis 17:7, 9, 13). These terms are used because it was a covenant in force for the benefit of both more remote and nearer generations. Its promises included and its law equally bound both during the whole state of the Mosaic economy. The right of the remotest generation was as much derived from Abraham and the covenant made with him, as was that of his immediate seed, and did not at all depend on the faithfulness of their immediate parents. Thus, the immediate seed of those Israelites that fell in the wilderness under the displeasure of God were made to inherit the land of Canaan by virtue of this covenant with Abraham. They never could have enjoyed it by virtue of their immediate parent's steadfastness in the covenant.

had to prove that the paedobaptists were wrong to establish a unity of substance between the Old and New Covenants and on this basis to take principles belonging to the Old Covenant and make them uniform although they were foreign to the New Covenant. This was a great challenge, because the unity of substance of the Covenant of Grace was seen as self-evident (something the Baptists also believed) and sufficient to justify the continuity of the principle of natural posterity through the identity of the substance between the two testaments (which was rejected by the Baptists).

For example, Francis Turretin, in defending the identity of substance between the Old and New Covenants on the basis of the unity of the Covenant of Grace, affirmed the perennial nature of the principle "I will be your God and the God of you posterity after you":

> Second, in particular, from all the parts of the Covenant of Grace which were the same in both cases. Such is the clause of the covenant that God will be our God and the God of our seed; for as it had already been proposed to Abraham (Gen. 17.7) and renewed to Moses in a vision (Ex. 3.15) and frequently in legislation, confirmed in the captivity and after it (Ezk. 36.28),

I suppose it cannot be denied that gross idolatry was a manifest and full breach of this covenant on the part of the idolater. Yet when the Israelites in Ezekiel's time became guilty of the vilest idolatries, the Lord still claims an interest in their children by virtue of this covenant (16:20, 21), [...] The children of the apostate Israelite were God's as well as those of his faithful servants. This could not have been if their covenant interest had depended on the good behaviour of immediate parents." *A Discourse of the Covenants*, p. 97-98.

This point is particularly important since paedobaptism depended entirely on the importation, under the New Covenant, of a principle belonging to the Abrahamic covenant; however the paedobaptists did not apply the principle of natural posterity given to Abraham in an honest and coherent way and applied it in a way which was foreign to the Abrahamic covenant as well as to the New Covenant. What is more, the paedobaptists did not explain why the natural descendents of Abraham were excluded from the Covenant (Mat. 21.43; Rom. 9.27ff.) while they were to be included in it in a permanent way (Gen. 17.7). Thus, the dispensationalists have a more generous conception of the grace granted to the natural posterity of Abraham, than that of the Presbyterians. We will compare the Presbyterian and Baptist understandings of the Abrahamic covenant in the next chapter.

so no other was proposed in the Covenant of Grace as the foundation of all blessings, spiritual as well as celestial (Mt. 22.32; 2 Cor 6.16; Rev 21.3).[18]

Thus, all paedobaptists considered that the children of believers had God as their God, at least in an external fashion, under the administration of the Covenant of Grace. Thomas Blake even published a treatise specifically on this question: *The Birth Priviledge: or, Covenant Holinesse of Beleevers and their Issue in the Time of the Gospel. Together with the Right of Infants to Baptisme* (1643).

Let us review. Because no man has been saved other than through the grace of God since the fall, the reformed considered that there had only one Covenant of Grace in the whole history of redemption. The Covenant of Grace was the substance by which seventeenth-century theologians united the Bible from whence came their paradigm: *one covenant under several administrations.* In establishing a distinction between the internal substance and the external administration of the Covenant of Grace, the Presbyterians managed to maintain the unity of this covenant while admitting a certain disparity between the different administrations. What is more, by separating the substance and administration, the paedobaptists introduced a notion of mixed nature within the Covenant of Grace by which they explained that "unconverted" people could be in the covenant without taking part in its substance while being hermetically contained in its administration. Finally, in considering the Old and New Covenants simply as administrations of the same covenant by insisting on the identity of their substance, the paedobaptists perpetuated a principle given to Abraham: "I will be your God and the God of your posterity." This principle allowed

---

[18] Francis Turretin, *Institutes of Elenctic Theology*, vol. 2, p. 195. Cf. also Thomas Goodwin, *A Discourse of Election*, p. 428ff. Goodwin attempts to explain that the "covenantal" privilege "I will be your God and the God of your posterity after you" was reserved for Abraham as "the father of all believers," but that it is also the privilege of all children of Abraham to also have their own posterity counted in the Covenant of Grace.

the paedobaptists to consider their children as members of the Covenant of Grace and, by making the distinction between the substance and the administration, they justified a legitimate place for them: that of the unregenerate who participate nevertheless in the Covenant of Grace and who receive the seal: formerly circumcision, now baptism.

This understanding of the Covenant of Grace was very widespread amongst the reformed theologians of the seventeenth century.

2.3. One Covenant under two administrations: a generalized model

The notions that we have just presented relating to the Covenant of Grace were implicit in all reformed theology of the sixteenth and seventeenth centuries. John Ball writes: "For manner of administration this Covenant is divers, as it pleased God in sundry manners to dispense it: but for substance it is one, the last, unchangeable and everlasting."[19] Ball fully endorses the fundamental distinction between the substance and the administration of the Covenant of Grace. A little further, in using the same distinction, Ball explains that the Pharisees were in the Covenant of Grace all the while being excluded from its substance:

> In respect of the externall administration of the Covenant they were counted the seed: but they walked not in the steps of the faith of Abraham, and therefore indeed and truth they were not the seed. [...] Further it is to be observed, that in all the seed the Covenant reacheth to Infants borne of the seed under the Covenant, which was the reason why they must receive the seale of the Covenant at eight dayes old. [20]

The paradigm *one covenant under two administrations* allowed Ball to affirm the mixed nature of the Covenant of Grace by isolating its external administration from its internal substance and

---

[19] John Ball, *A Treatise of the Covenant of Grace*, p. 23
[20] *Ibid.*, p. 51f.

enabled him to import under the New Covenant a principle of posterity, belonging, according to him, to the substance of the Covenant of Grace. Ball did not affirm the mixed nature of the Covenant of Grace in an implicit way, but he did so explicitly:

> God as an absolute Soveraigne hath right and authority over all men: but in a certaine and peculiar reason they are called his people, who receive his Commandement, and acknowledge him to be their Lord and Saviour. And these be of two sorts; for God doth make his Covenant with some externally, calling them by his Word, and sealing them by his Sacraments, and they by profession of faith and receiving of the Sacraments oblige themselves to the condition required: and thus all members of the visible Church be in Covenant. With others God doth make his Covenant effectually, writing his Law in their hearths by his holy Spirit, and they freely and from the hearth give up themselves unto the Lord, in all things to be ruled and guided by him. And thus God hath contracted Covenant with the faithfull only. The first fort are the people of God outwardly or openly, having all things externall and pertaining to the outward administration. The second are the people of God inward or in secret, whom certainly and distinctly the Lord only knoweth. [21]

The substance/administration distinction found in the Presbyterian understanding of the Covenant of Grace allowed Ball to affirm that two categories of people found themselves in the Covenant of Grace: regenerated and the unregenerate. Thomas Blake was even more explicit than Ball: in his treatise *Vindiciae Foederis*, he devoted an entire chapter to demonstrating the mixed nature of the Covenant of Grace administrated under the New Covenant; he entitled this chapter: *"The Covenant of Grace in Gospel-times admits Christians in profession in a state of unregeneration, and is not limited in the bounds of it to the Elect*

---

[21] *Ibid.*, p. 202f.

regenerate."[22] In this chapter Blake explains that the Covenant of Grace is first visible, external and inefficacious: "First, That Covenant between God and man [...] is a Covenant onely visibly entred, and doth not require any inward reall change, or work upon the soul to the being of it."[23] He pursues his argumentation in justifying the doctrine of the visible Church which, according to him, corresponds to national Churches. He bases his claim on the Great Commission from Mathew 28.19 to explain his point:

> That which a whole Nation in Gods ordinary way of administration is in a capacitie to attain and enter into, is onely a Covenant professed, visibly entred [sic] upon, and doth not require any inward change, or work upon the soul to the being of it; this is plain, it cannot be expected in Gods ordinary way, that a Nation should be brought forth at one all really holy and sanctified [...] But whole Nations are in a capacity (in Gods ordinary way of working) to enter into this Covenant, as is plain in the Text; The whole of the Nation is in their commission where they come, and in many Nations it hath had happy successe.[24]

This paragraph demonstrates to what degree Presbyterian federalism was the basis for their ecclesiology and how the distinction between the substance and the administration (*God's ordinary way of working*) of the covenant justified the national model of the Reformed Church. Blake continues his demonstration of the mixed nature of the Covenant of Grace by using the parable of the wedding feast in Mathew 22.1-13; Blake believes that the man who was not wearing wedding garments corresponds to the unregenerate who are in the Covenant of Grace.[25] He supports his

---

[22] Thomas Blake, *Vindiciae Foederis; or A Treatise of the Covenant of God Entered With Man-Kinde, In the Severa Kindes and Degrees of it*, London, Printed for Abel Roper, 1653, p. 189.
[23] *Ibid.*, p. 193.
[24] *Ibid.*, p. 194.
[25] *Ibid.*, p. 197.

argument using Hebrews 10.29 to prove that all those who are in the covenant are not necessarily saved:

> Where we see those that are sanctified with the blood of the Covenant do tread under foot the Son of God, and count his blood an unholy thing, have an esteem of it, as that which is common, and never devoted at all to God. These must needs be granted to be wicked, yet cannot be denied to be in Covenant, being sanctified with the blood of the Covenant. [26]

Blake once again defends the mixed nature of the Church by trying to prove that the New Testament names as believers, as saints, as disciples and as Christians people who are not regenerated. For example, he considers that the five thousand men converted at Pentecost belonged to the visible Church and that, although they all professed the faith, they were not all regenerated. Simon the magician would be an example of one of these believers who were not saved.[27] Blake also gives the example of the non-believing spouse who is called a saint by virtue of the believer (1 Co 7.14); he thereby deduces that the New Testament does not apply qualifiers and substantives used to designate those who are in the Covenant of Grace exclusively to the regenerated.[28]

---

[26] *Ibid.*, p. 198. Blake is very careful to explain what the sanctification of the "unconverted" is within the Covenant of Grace; it does not refer to the purification from their sins. We believe that Blane's exegesis is faulty, because we believe that the verb ἡγιάσθῃ (has been sanctified) refers not to "he who has trampled the Son of God underfoot, who has treated as an unholy thing the blood of the covenant" , but to the covenant which was sanctified by the blood of Christ. The translation of this verse should be: "How much more severely do you think someone deserves to be punished who has trampled the Son of God underfoot, who has treated as an unholy thing the blood of the covenant that sanctified them, and who has insulted the Spirit of grace?" This verse is talking about apostates and not members of the covenant; this verse does not approve the idea that the New Covenant would be "transgressable" by its members. We will come back to this in Chapter 4 which deals with the New Covenant.

[27] *Ibid.*, p. 206.

[28] *Ibid.*

He concludes by explaining that those who confine the covenant to the regenerated are confusing the covenant itself with its condition:

> This restriction of the Covenant (to shut out all non-Regenerate) makes an utter confusion between the Covenant itself, and the conditions of it; or (if that expression do not please) the Covenant itself and the duties required in it, between our entrance into Covenant, and our observation of it, or waling up in faithfulnesse to it. [29]

This understanding of the Covenant of Grace was officially integrated in the standards of Westminster. We have already quoted the Confession of Westminster to this effect, but the catechism of the same name also articulated this theology. For example, in question 33 of the Larger Catechism of Westminster, we find the basis of the Covenant of Grace as a unique covenant administered in different ways:

> Q. Was the Covenant of Grace always administered after one and the same manner?
> A. The Covenant of Grace was not always administered after the same manner, but the administrations of it under the Old Testament were different from those under the New.

Based on this, in question 166, the mixed nature of the Covenant of Grace is implied in invoking the concept of the visible Church (external administration) and the principle of posterity is explicitly affirmed:

> Q. Unto whom is baptism to be administered?
> A. Baptism is not to be administered to any that are out of the visible church, till they profess their faith in Christ; and obedience to him; but infants descended from parents, either

---

[29] *Ibid.*, p. 209. We could already see, in the seventeenth century, a natural tendency of Presbyterianism toward covenantal nomism which has become an important controversy amongst today's paedobaptists where fidelity towards the covenant replaces faith, rendering the Covenant of Grace conditional.

both or but one of them professing faith in Christ, and obedience to him, are, in that respect, within the covenant and to be baptized.

In considering the Old and New Covenants not as separate covenants but simply as two administrations of the same covenant, their differences were reduced to being of a qualitative nature. Thus, Peter Bulkeley compared the Covenant of Grace before Christ and the Covenant of Grace after Christ only in terms of degree:

> Wherein stands the difference between the old and new manner of the dispensation of the Covenant of Grace. It stands principally in foure things. 1. One more burdensome, another more easie. 2. One more darke, the other more cleare. 3. One more weake, the other more lively and strong. 4. In regard of the extent of the dispensation, one dispensed to that one people of the Jews, the other to all Nations. [30]

By defining the Covenant of Grace as being one covenant under several administrations, the very nature of the Old and New Covenants was predetermined. Most paedobaptist theologians reduced the differences between these two "administrations" not to differences in substance, but to qualitative differences. Turretin represents well the point of view of the paedobaptist theologians of his time in writing:

> The orthodox maintain that the difference between the Old and New Testaments (broadly considered) is only accidental, not essential (as to the circumstance and manner and degree of the thing); not as to the thing itself, which was the same in each. [31]

These differences of degree were explained only under the angle of chronology: before Christ and after Christ. The paedobaptists spoke of the Covenant of Grace *"administered in the time of the*

---

[30] Peter Bulkeley, *The Gospel Covenant; or The Covenant of Grace Opened*, p. 105ff.
[31] Francis Turretin, *Institutes of Elenctic Theology*, vol. 2, p. 237.

law, and in the time of the gospel"³² or of the Covenant of Grace
"before and after the coming of Christ."³³ For them, the differences
between the Old and New Covenants could be explained
chronologically and not in substance. The same thing is found with
Herman Witsius:

> But yet you will say, something is here promised to be obtained
> by virtue of the New Covenant which the old could not give, in
> the place of which the new was substituted on account of its
> imperfections. I answer: the apostle does not here oppose the
> Covenant of Grace, as it is dispensed after the coming of Christ,
> to the same Covenant of Grace, as it was dispensed before: but
> opposes the Covenant of Grace, as in its full efficacy under the
> New Testament, to the national covenant made with the
> Israelites at mount Sinai; and as a spiritual covenant to a
> typical.³⁴

We could continue to demonstrate the particularities of
seventeenth-century Presbyterian federalism, but we believe we
have clearly demonstrated the fact that all of these particularities
were fundamentally attached to the *one covenant under two
administrations* paradigm and to the fundamental distinction
between the substance and the administration of the Covenant of
Grace. We will now present another understanding of the Covenant
of Grace which became entrenched, we believe, in the development
of the reformed way of thought and which revolutionized
ecclesiology.

---

³² *The Westminster Confession of Faith.* VII, V.
³³ Peter Bulkeley, *The Gospel Covenant; or The Covenant of Grace Opened*, p.
102
³⁴ Herman Witsius, *The Economy of the Covenants*, vol. 2, p. 336.

3. THE COVENANT OF GRACE AS SEEN BY BAPTISTS: A COVENANT REVEALED PROGRESSIVELY AND FORMALLY CONCLUDED

3.1. Unity above all

The Baptists were very concerned for maintaining unity with their paedobaptist brothers. Most of them were very peace-loving; think of Nehemiah Coxe who says that he hesitated a long time before publishing his treatise in order to avoid controversy with the paedobaptists whom he recognized as brothers loving the Lord Jesus.[35] Let us also think of the appendix that the Baptists joined to the publication of the Second London Confession of Faith where, several times, they express their desire to maintain good relations with the paedobaptists regardless of their divergences of opinion on the question of baptism:

> [W]e have also industriously endeavored to manifest, that in the fundamental Articles of Christianity we mind the same things, and have therefore expressed our belief in the same words, that have on the like occasion been spoken by other societies of Christians before us. [...]

> And although we do differ from our brethren who are paedobaptists in the subject and administration of Baptism, and such other circumstances as have a necessary dependence on our observance of that ordinance, [...] yet we would not be from hence misconstrued, as if the discharge of our own consciences herein, did anyway disoblige or alienate our affections, or conversation from any others that fear the Lord. [...]

> These things we have mentioned as having a direct reference unto the controversy between our brethren and us. Other things that are more abstruse and prolix, which are frequently introduced into this controversy, but do not necessarily concern

---

[35] Cf. Nehemiah Coxe, *A Discourse of the Covenants*, p. 30-31.

it we have purposely avoided that the distance between us and
our brethren may not be by us made more wide. For it is our
duty and concern so far as possible for us (retaining a good
conscience towards God) to seek a more entire agreement and
reconciliation with them. [36]

In rejecting the paedobaptist model of the Covenant of Grace,
the Baptists did not want to do as the Socinians, who had rejected
the Covenant of Grace itself and reformed theology as a whole.
They wanted to distance themselves from the latter and identify
with reformed orthodoxy. The Baptists maintained unity with the
Presbyterians by affirming the unity of the Covenant of Grace.
Baptist theology subscribed fully to the notion of their being only
one Covenant of Grace in the Bible, which brings together all who
are saved as one people. The Confession of 1689 clearly teaches
this doctrine.

First, in Chapter 7, on The Covenant of God, in paragraph 2:
"Moreover, man having brought himself under the curse of the law
by his fall, it pleased the Lord to make a covenant of grace, wherein
He freely offers unto sinners life and salvation by Jesus Christ." The
Baptists considered that the Covenant of Grace started immediately
after the Fall and that the substance of this covenant, even under the
Old Testament, was salvation through faith in Jesus Christ.
Paragraph 3 leaves no doubt that the Baptists believed that the
Gospel started with Adam: "This covenant is revealed in the gospel;
first of all to Adam in the promise of salvation by the seed of the
woman, and afterwards by farther steps, until the full discovery
thereof was completed in the New Testament." In Chapter 11,
paragraph 6, regarding justification, the Baptists explicitly refute
Socinian theology: "The justification of believers under the Old
Testament was, in all these respects, one and the same with the
justification of believers under the New Testament." Since the
substance of the Covenant of Grace was salvation through faith in

---

[36] The appendix to the Confession of 1689 is published in Fred Malone's, *The
Baptism of Disciples Alone*, Cape Coral, Founders Press, 2003, p. 253ff. The
passages cited here are from pages 253, 254 and 263.

Jesus Christ, by stating the uniformity of justification by faith in both testaments, they implicitly affirmed the unity of the Covenant of Grace in both testaments. Then, in Chapter 21, paragraph 1, Of Christian Liberty and the Liberty of Conscience, the Baptists maintained that the substance of salvation was the same under both covenants: "[...] All of that was common also to believers under the law in terms of its substance."

Thirty years before the publication of the 1689, Henry Lawrence, in his treatise on baptism, affirmed the unity of the Covenant of Grace under the two testaments:

> I confess there are some things of common equity, the rule of life was the same then that now, and the same Christ that now is, was the salvation of the elect, such things therefore as are of such common nature, may be illustrated and inferred from one Testament to another.[37]

Edward Hutchinson, for his part, extensively quoted John Owen in order to demonstrate the unity and continuity of the Church of the Old and New Testaments. Since the Church is the people of the Covenant of Grace and since there is only one people of God in all of the Bible, there was necessarily only one Covenant of Grace before and after Christ to assemble this people under the same covenant:

> Hence it was, that at the coming of the Messiah there was not one Church taken away and another set up in the room thereof, but the Church continued the same in those that were the children of Abraham according to the faith. The Christian Church is not another Church, but the very same that was before the coming of Christ, having the same faith with it, and interested in the same Covenant.[38]

---

[37] Henry Lawrence, *Of Baptism*, London, Printed by F. Macock, 1659 (1646), p. 83
[38] Quoted by Edward Hutchinson, *A Treatise Concerning the Covenant and Baptism*, p. 33.

By using Owen's words, Hutchinson demonstrated that the credobaptists shared the same conviction as the paedobaptists regarding the unity of the Covenant of Grace. The Baptists had this conviction from the beginning; John Spilsbury, who was the pastor of the first Calvinist Baptist Church and who published the oldest treatise of Baptist covenant theology, affirms: "The Church of God under the old Testament, and that now under the new, for nature are one, in reference to the Elect of God, called to the faith, and by the Spirit of grace united to Christ, as the branches to their vine."[39]

Although the Baptists believed in the unity of the Covenant of Grace, like their interlocutors, and though they wanted to maintain unity with them, they rejected the *one covenant under two administrations* model.

3.2. Rejection of the Presbyterian model

The Baptists saw a unity of substance in the Covenant of Grace from Genesis to Revelation, but they didn't see this same unity between the Old and the New Covenants. They therefore did not accept the idea that those two covenants were two administrations of a same covenant. Nehemiah Coxe expresses this fundamental Baptist conviction well: ""[...] the Old Covenant and the new differ in substance and not only in the manner of their admin-istration."[40] Consequently, none of them endorsed the theology of one Covenant of Grace under two administrations.[41] The rejection or

---

[39] John Spilsbury, *A Treatise Concerning the Lawfull Subject of Baptisme*, London, By me J.S., 1643, p. 20.

[40] Nehemiah Coxe, *A Discourse of the Covenants*, p. 30

[41] It is interesting to note that John Smyth supported the doctrine of one Covenant of Grace under two administrations. This indicates that the General Baptists and the Particular Baptists did not arrive at credobaptism through the same reasoning nor based on the same theological foundation. Smyth writes: "Remember that there be alwaies a difference put betwixt the covenant of grace; and the manner of dispensing it, which is twofold: the form of administring the covenant before the death of Christ, which is called the old testament; and the forme of administring the covenant since the death of Christ which is called the new Testament of the kingdome of heaven." *Principles and Inferences concerning the Visible Church,*

acceptance of this model (one covenant under two administrations) had important repercussions on all the rest of covenant theology. John Owen writes: "Here then arises a difference of no small importance, namely, whether these [the Old and New Covenants] are indeed two distinct covenants, as to the essence and substance of them, or only different ways of the dispensation and administration of the same covenant."[42] The understanding of the nature and the function of the Old and New Covenants depended totally on this question.

In comparing the confessions of faith, it becomes evident that the Baptists completely rejected the paedobaptist model of the Covenant of Grace:

1689 (7.3)	Savoy (7.5)	Westminster (7.5-6)
This Covenant is revealed in the Gospel; first of all to Adam in the promise of Salvation by the seed of the woman, and afterwards by farther steps, until the full discovery thereof was completed in the New Testament; and it is founded in that Eternal Covenant transaction, that was between the Father	Although this covenant hath been differently and variously administered in respect of ordinances and institutions in the time of the law, and since the coming of Christ in the flesh; yet for the substance and efficacy of it, to all its spiritual and saving ends, it is one and the same; upon	This covenant was differently administered in the time of the law, and in the time of the gospel: under the law, it was administered by promises, prophecies, sacrifices, circumcision, the paschal lamb, and other types and ordinances delivered to the people of the Jews, all foresigni-

---

1607; quoted in: Paul S. Fiddes, *Tracks and Traces, Baptist Identity in Church and Theology*, Eugene, OR, Wipf & Stock, 2003, p. 26. We must, however, admit that certain Calvinist Baptist authors sometimes spoke of "the administrations of the Covenant of Grace," but what they meant by this terminology was different from paedobaptist theology.

[42] John Owen, *An Exposition of Hebrews 8:6-13*, p. 179.

| and the Son, about the Redemption of the Elect; and it is alone by the Grace of this Covenant, that all of the posterity of fallen Adam, that ever were saved, did obtain life and a blessed immortality; Man being now utterly incapable of acceptance with God upon those terms, on which Adam stood in his state of innocency. | the account of which various dispens- ations, it is called the Old and New Testament. | fying Christ to come; which were, for that time, sufficient and efficacious, through the operation of the Spirit, to instruct and build up the elect in faith in the promised Messiah by whom they had full remission of sins, and eternal salvation; and is called the Old Testament.

Under the gospel, when Christ, the substance, was exhibited, […] and is called the New Testament. There are not therefore two covenants of grace, differing in substance, but one and the same, under various dispensations. |
|---|---|---|

This is the most discordant passage of the confessions of faith. Knowing that the Baptists made every effort to follow the Westminster standards as much as possible when they wrote their confession of faith, the originality of their formulation of the Covenant of Grace is highly significant. It is obvious that the authors of the 1689 completely avoided any formulation reminiscent of the *"one covenant under two administrations"* model that we find in the other two confessions of faith. This absence must be interpreted as a rejection of the theology behind this formulation and not as an omission or an attempt at originality. The Baptists' opinion regarding the Presbyterian model of the Covenant of Grace concords exactly with that of John Owen who states it thus: "[...] we may consider that Scripture does plainly and expressly make mention of two testaments, or covenants, and distinguish between them in such a way, that what is spoken can hardly be accommodated to a twofold administration of the same covenant."[43]

3.3. The affirmation of the Baptist model

We have just seen what seventeenth-century Baptist federalism was not. Let us now examine what it was.

3.3.1. The Covenant of Grace revealed progressively

By rejecting the notion of a covenant of grace under two admin- istrations, the Baptists were in fact rejecting only half of this concept: they accepted, as we have previously seen, the notion of one single Covenant of Grace in both testaments, but they refused the idea of the two administrations. For the Baptists, there was only one Covenant of Grace which was revealed from the Fall in a progressive way until its full revelation and conclusion in the New Covenant. This model is clearly expressed in Chapter 7 paragraph 3 of the Confession of 1689: "This covenant is revealed in the gospel; first of all to Adam in the promise of salvation by the seed of the woman, and afterwards by farther steps, until the full discovery thereof was completed in the New Testament."

Upon first impression, this definition does not seem to be radically different from that of the paedobaptists since they also recognized the progressive revelation of the Covenant of Grace. However, in studying Baptist theology in its historical context, it becomes evident that this definition of the Covenant of Grace had a

---

[43] John Owen, *An Exposition of Hebrews 8:6-13*, p. 186.

meaning that was very specific and fundamentally different from the paedobaptist understanding.

The first particularity is found in the difference between the notion of administration and that of revelation. The Baptists believed that before the arrival of the New Covenant, the Covenant of Grace was not formally given, but only announced and promised (revealed). This distinction is fundamental to the federalism of the 1689. Nehemiah Coxe, the protagonist of this confession of faith, firmly maintains this distinction between the revelation and the administration:

> It must also be noted that although the Covenant of Grace was revealed this far to Adam, yet we see in all this there was no formal and express covenant transaction with him. Even less was the Covenant of Grace established with him as a public person or representative of any kind. But as he obtained interest for himself alone by his own faith in the grace of God revealed in this way, so must those of his posterity that are saved. [44]

This specification is highly significant and plays a determining role in Baptist federalism. For Coxe, the Covenant of Grace was not concluded when God revealed it to Adam. John Owen explains why the Covenant of Grace could not be considered a formal covenant before the establishment of the New Covenant, but was confined to the stage of a promise:

> It lacked its solemn confirmation and establishment, by the blood of the only sacrifice which belonged to it. Before this was done in the death of Christ, it had not the formal nature of a covenant or a testament, as our apostle proves, Heb. 9:15-23. For neither, as he shows in that place, would the law given at Sinai have been a covenant, had it not been confirmed with the

---

[44] Nehemiah Coxe, *A Discourse of the Covenants*, p. 57. John Ball also spoke of the different stages of the Covenant of Grace as promised and then established, but he did not apply the same theological consequences to this nuance as the Baptists.

blood of sacrifices. To that end the promise was not before a formal and solemn covenant. [45]

The distinction between the revelation and the administration of the Covenant of Grace finds its whole meaning when the second element of Baptist federalism is added to it, that is to say, the full revelation of the Covenant of Grace in the New Covenant. If the Westminster federalism can be summarized in *"one covenant under two administrations,"* that of the 1689 would be *"one covenant revealed progressively and concluded formally under the New Covenant."*

3.3.2. The Covenant of Grace fully revealed in the New Covenant

The Baptists believed that no covenant preceding the New Covenant was the Covenant of Grace. Before the arrival of the New Covenant, the Covenant of Grace was at the stage of promise. According to Benjamin Keach, the expression "the covenants of the promise" that can be found in Ephesians 2.12 refers back to the Covenant of Grace.[46] The promise in question was the Covenant of Grace. If we are talking about a promise, this implies that it was not yet accomplished and was not yet in the form of a testament or a covenant. The Baptists believed that the New Covenant was the accomplishment of the promise, or in other words, the accomplishment of the Covenant of Grace. This doctrine is expressed in the following way in the 1689: "This covenant is revealed in the gospel; first of all to Adam [...] and afterwards by farther steps, until the full discovery thereof was completed in the New Testament." The New Testament brings the full revelation of the Covenant of Grace since the New Covenant is its accomplishment. The Baptists considered that the New Covenant and it alone was the Covenant of Grace.[47]

---

[45] John Owen, *An Exposition of Hebrews 8:6-13,* p. 185.

[46] Benjamin Keach, *The Display of Glorious Grace,* p. 182.

[47] In Baptist theology we find an equivalency between the Covenant of Grace and the New Covenant, and this, from the First London Confession of faith in 1644, in paragraph 10 where we read: "Jesus Christ is made the mediator of the new and

If the New Covenant did not exist before Jesus Christ, while the Covenant of Grace existed before the coming of the Messiah, does this not mean that both covenants are distinct? The New Covenant did not exist as a covenant before Jesus Christ; however it did exist as a promise (cf. Jer. 31.31). The Covenant of Grace revealed to Adam, then to Abraham, was the New Covenant promised. Therefore, before Jesus Christ, the New Covenant did not exist, but the Covenant of Grace, did not exist as a formal covenant either. John Spilsbury affirmed this notion: "Again, it's called the promise, and not the Covenant; and we know that every promise is not a covenant: there being a large difference between a promise and a covenant.[48] Spilsbury speaks of the Covenant of Grace that God revealed to Abraham and he declares that at this stage, it was not yet a formal covenant, but a promise.

This distinction: (revealed/concluded) summarized the difference between the Covenant of Grace in the Old Testament and the Covenant of Grace in the New Testament. In the Old, it was revealed, in the New, it was concluded (fully revealed according to the expression of the 1689). John Owen comes to exactly the same understanding in his exegesis of Hebrews 8.6 where we read: "But in fact the ministry Jesus has received is as superior to theirs as the covenant of which he is mediator is superior to the old one, since the New Covenant is established on better promises." Owen concentrates

---

everlasting covenant of grace." The expression *"the new and everlasting covenant of grace"* includes both the Covenant of Grace and the New Covenant. Thus, there is a distinction, without separation between the Covenant of Grace and the New Covenant. John Bunyan also uses the expressions "Covenant of Grace" and "New Covenant" interchangeably, cf. "The Doctrine of the Law and Grace Unfolded," *The Works of John Bunyan*, Carlisle, Banner of Truth Trust, 1991, volume 1, p. 540s. Let us note that the paedobaptists also saw an equivalency between the Covenant of Grace and the New Covenant. In paragraph 4, Chapter 7 of the Confession of Westminster for example: "This covenant of grace is frequently set forth in Scripture by the name of a testament, in reference to the death of Jesus Christ [...] " However, the rest of their theology demonstrates that they perceived the New Covenant as an administration of the Covenant of Grace and not as the Covenant of Grace in and of itself.

[48] John Spilsbury, *A Treatise Concerning the Lawfull Subject of Baptisme*, p. 26.

on the verb νομοθετέω (established) to explain the difference between the Covenant of Grace before and after Jesus Christ.

> This is the meaning of the word νενομοθέτηται: [...] "reduced into a fixed state of a law or ordinance." All the obedience required in it, all the worship appointed by it, all the privileges exhibited in it, and the grace administered with them, are all given for a statute, law, and ordinance to the church. That which before lay hid in promises, in many things obscure, [...] was now brought to light; and that covenant which had invisibly, in the way of promise, put forth its efficacy under types and shadows, was now solemnly sealed, ratified, and confirmed, in the death and resurrection of Christ. *It had before the confirmation of promise, which is an oath; it had now the confirmation of a covenant, which is blood.* That which before had no visible, outward worship, proper and peculiar to it, is now made the only rule and instrument of worship to the whole church, nothing being to be admitted in that respect but what belongs to it, and is appointed by it. The apostle intends this by νενομοθέτηται, the "legal establishment' of the New Covenant, with all the ordinances of its worship. On this the other covenant was disannulled and removed; and not only the covenant itself, but all that system of sacred worship in accordance with which it was administered. [...] When the New Covenant was given out only in the way of a promise, it was consistent with a form of worship, rites and ceremonies, and those composed into a yoke of bondage which belonged not to it. And as these, they were inconsistent with it when it was completed as a covenant; for then all the worship of the church was to proceed from it, and to be conformed to it.[49]

Before the establishment (νενομοθέτηται) of the New Covenant, the Covenant of Grace did not have a concrete manifestation, any cultus or ceremony; it was not a covenant, but a promise revealed in an obscure manner under temporary types and shadows: "These are a shadow of the things that were to come; the reality, however, is

---

[49] John Owen, *An Exposition of Hebrews 8:6-13,* p. 173-4. Italics added.

found in Christ." (Col 2.17). Before Christ, the Covenant of Grace was announced; after Christ, it was decreed (νενομοθέτηται). [50]

Owen adds to this by saying that the Covenant of Grace, as a formal covenant, exists only in the New Covenant. The Covenant of Grace, in this specific sense, was not given to Adam or to Abraham: "[...] this covenant, as here considered, is not understood the promise of grace given to Adam absolutely; nor that to Abraham, which contained the substance and matter of it, the grace exhibited in it, but not the complete form of it as a covenant." [51] God did not conclude the Covenant of Grace with Adam any more than He did with Abraham; he revealed the substance of the covenant to them, but it was only concluded through Jesus Christ, in his sacrifice. Nehemiah Coxe affirms the same thing: "[...] in the wise counsel of God Things were so ordered that the full revelation of the Covenant of Grace, the actual accomplishment of its great promises, and its being filled up with ordinances proper to it, should succeed the covenant made with Israel after the flesh." [52] This understanding was radically different from that of the majority of paedobaptists in the seventeenth century.

Benjamin Keach, one of the main Baptist theologians of the second half of the seventeenth century, ratifies this view of the Covenant of Grace when he describes its four sequences: 1.It was first decreed in past eternity, 2. It was secondly revealed to man after the Fall of Adam and Eve, 3. It was executed and confirmed by Christ in his death and resurrection, 4. It becomes effective for its members when they are joined to Christ through faith. [53] The particularity of this *ordo salutis* is the distinction between the revelation and the execution of the Covenant of Grace. Those who

---

[50] Jeffrey Johnson, after having thoroughly examined the fallacies of Presbyterian federalism, comes to the same conclusion: "Before Christ the Covenant of Grace was promised. After Christ the Covenant of Grace was established." *The Fatal Flaw of the Theology Behind Infant Baptism*, p. 247.

[51] John Owen, *An Exposition of Hebrews 8:6-13,* p. 239.

[52] Nehemiah Coxe, *A Discourse of the Covenants*, p. 91.

[53] Benjamin Keach, *The Everlasting Covenant*, London, Printed for H. Barnard, 1693, p. 17.

were saved before Christ were saved because of an oath; those who were saved after Him were saved because of a covenant. The Epistle to the Hebrews makes this distinction when it bases the faith of believers of the Old Covenant on the oath that God made to Abraham (Heb. 6.17-18). However, the assurance of the believers of the New Covenant rests on a testament that is the achieved work of Christ (Heb. 7-9). We also find this distinction in the relationship between justification and divine justice as set forth in Romans 3:

> [25] God presented Christ as a sacrifice of atonement, through the shedding of his blood—to be received by faith. He did this to demonstrate his righteousness, because in his forbearance he had left the sins committed beforehand unpunished— [26] he did it to demonstrate his righteousness at the present time, so as to be just and the one who justifies those who have faith in Jesus. (Rom. 3.25-26)

The time of God's patience is situated between the fall of man and the death of His son; this is the period where the Covenant of Grace was not formally concluded in the blood of Christ. In establishing this alliance, God has finally manifested that He is just, even if he had been justifying the impious since the creation of the world.

Galatians chapter 3, verses 17 and 18 is another passage that clearly indicates that the Covenant of Grace was first presented in the form of a promise and not as a formal covenant.[54]

---

[54] Nevertheless, this passage uses legal terminology to indicate that a testament was concluded between God and Abraham (διαθήκην προκεκυρωμένην ὑπὸ τοῦ θεου). However, Paul designates this testament and this heritage as a promise twice. This indicates that the Covenant of Grace was revealed in the Abrahamic covenant all the while being distinct from it. The Abrahamic covenant revealed the Covenant of Grace, but was not formally the Covenant of Grace. The test says that it is through the promise that God gave his grace and not through the covenant. We will examine this point in further detail in Chapter 3.

3.3.3. The Covenant of Grace and the Old Covenant

The Baptist understanding of the Covenant of Grace completely changed the perception of the Old Covenant. The paedobaptists saw the aforementioned as a formal administration of the Covenant of Grace; but as soon as it was affirmed that there was no formal establishment of the Covenant of Grace before the New Covenant, one could no longer see the Old Covenant as an administration of the Covenant of Grace. If the Baptists didn't see the Old Covenant as a covenant of grace, how did they see it? We will see the answer to this question more specifically in our chapter dedicated to the Old Covenant; for now, we will be content to highlight the fact that the Baptists saw the Old Covenant as a radically different covenant from the Covenant of Grace and as a covenant that, contrary to the New Covenant, did not offer salvation. In this connection, Owen's thinking corresponded once again to that of the Baptists.

> If reconciliation and salvation by Christ were to be obtained not only under the Old Covenant, but by virtue of it, then it must be the same for substance with the new. But this is not so; for no reconciliation with God nor salvation could be obtained by virtue of the Old Covenant, or the administration of it, as our apostle disputes at large [...]
> As therefore I have showed in what sense the Covenant of Grace is called "the New Covenant," in this distinction and opposition, so I will propose various things which relate to the nature of the first covenant, which manifest it to have been a distinct covenant, and not a mere administration of the Covenant of Grace[55].

Thomas Patient expresses the same conviction: "Now I come in the next place to prove that the Covenant of Circumcision is no Covenant of Eternal Life."[56] According to this understanding, no

---

[55] John Owen, *An Exposition of Hebrews 8:6-13,* p. 187, 188.
[56] Thomas Patient, *The Doctrine of Baptism, And the Distinction of the Covenants,* London, Printed by Henry Hills, 1654. This affirmation is found at the beginning of chapter 9 of this non-paginated work.

one was ever saved by virtue of the Old Covenant since the substance of the Old Covenant was not the Covenant of Grace.

We have already seen that the Baptist reading of the Covenant of Grace (one covenant revealed progressively and formally concluded under the New Covenant) was explained by the exegesis of Hebrews 8.6: before the New Covenant, the Covenant of Grace was only revealed, when the New Covenant was introduced, it was νενομοθέτηται. This verb is used only twice in the Holy Scriptures; once to speak of the promulgation of the Old Covenant (Heb. 7.11) and a second time to relate the promulgation of the New Covenant (Heb. 8.6). These two covenants were established (νενομοθέτηται) on two completely different foundations. The first was established (νενομοθέτηται) on the Levitical priesthood with the blood of rams and calves (Heb. 9.18-19), whereas the second was founded (νενομοθέτηται) on an eternal priesthood in accordance with the order of Melchizedek and with the very blood of Christ (Heb. 9.12). How could two covenants with such different foundations have the same substance? Is it not the goal of the author of the Epistle to the Hebrews to demonstrate that the Old Covenant was but a shadow of what was to come, a typological covenant, temporary and earthly while the reality is to be found in the New Covenant in Jesus Christ? At least, this is how the Baptist pastor Edward Hutchinson understood this epistle: "For the old house, or Jewish Church was not intended to abide for ever, but to the time of reformation, then the law must be changed, the priesthood chang'd, the priviledges and ordinances chang'd, the seed chang'd, yea the Covenant chang'd."[57] Nehemiah Coxe summarizes the relationship between the Covenant of Grace and the Old Covenant as follows: "But the truth is, despite the relationship this covenant has to the Covenant of Grace, it yet remains distinct from it."[58]

The Baptists did not support a theology with Socinian tendencies wherein the salvation of the believers of the Old Testament would have been different from that of New Testament believers, such as:

---

[57]Edward Hutchinson, *A Treatise Concerning the Covenant and Baptism*, p. 40
[58] Nehemiah Coxe, *A Discourse of the Covenants*, p. 93.

one salvation through works and one salvation through faith. They were always careful not to affirm such a thing. While they denied the idea that the Old Covenant offered salvation through grace, they stated that all those who were saved under the Old Covenant were saved by the grace of salvation in Jesus Christ. This doctrine is clear in the Confession of 1689.

> Although the price of redemption was not actually paid by Christ till after his incarnation, yet the virtue, efficacy, and benefit thereof were communicated to the elect in all ages, successively from the beginning of the world, in and by those promises, types, and sacrifices wherein he was revealed, and signified to be the seed which should bruise the serpent's head; and the Lamb slain from the foundation of the world, being the same yesterday, and today and for ever.[59]

The Baptist model of the Covenant of Grace allowed for the coherent affirmation of this doctrine. According to this model, a progressive revelation of the Covenant of Grace before its establishment was considered. This progressive revelation started with Adam, continued with Noah, then with Abraham and his descendants. Thus, the Baptists could state that the Old Covenant did not give salvation, all the while affirming that salvation was given under the Old Covenant. This understanding can be summarized in this way: salvation was given under the Old Covenant, but not by virtue of the Old Covenant; during the time period of the Old Covenant but not by the Old Covenant. Edward Hutchinson writes:

> But surely that Covenant made with Abraham and his natural seed called the Covenant of Circumcision, or Covenant of the Law was not the Covenant of Eternal life and salvation, which was made with all the elect in Christ upon the condition of faith

---

[59] This is from paragraph 6 of Chapter 8. This paragraph is identical to the one in the Westminster Confession, which shows that the divergence between Presbyterian and Baptist federalism was not regarding the unity of the Covenant of Grace as such, but rather in its relationship with the Old and New Covenants.

[...] though there was also grace in it, as there was in all the Covenants that God ever made with men—yet we say, it was a distinct Covenant, and therefore called the old Covenant, and the Covenant of Grace the new Covenant.[60]

The Abrahamic Covenant, the Sinaitic Covenant and the Davidic Covenant were not the Covenant of Grace, nor administrations of it; however, the Covenant of Grace was revealed under these various covenants. The Epistle to the Hebrews seems to sanction this understanding, particularly this passage: "For this reason Christ is the mediator of a New Covenant, that those who are called may receive the promised eternal inheritance—now that he has died as a ransom to set them free from the sins committed under the first covenant." (Heb. 9.15).

The first covenant did not redeem transgressions; consequently it did not offer the forgiveness of sins. However, the believers under this covenant received the forgiveness of their sins and the heritage of salvation in Jesus Christ, something which is shown through the conjugation of the verb to call (κεκλημένοι) in the perfect tense. Those who were called before Christ paid for their transgressions received the eternal inheritance and those who continue to be called since that event receive this same promised inheritance. As a result, all those who were saved since the creation of the world were saved by virtue of the New Covenant which was in effect as a promise even before it was an accomplished covenant. Owen writes: "I will take here for granted, that no man was ever saved but by virtue of the New Covenant, and the mediation of Christ in that respect."[61]

Instead of considering that the New Covenant was in effect before it was concluded, certain paedobaptists stated that Christ was also the mediator of the Old Covenant and therefore justified the efficacy of grace by this covenant. This was the case of Thomas Blake who writes: "In severall things there is a full agreement between these Covenants. [...] *In the Mediatour Christ Jesus*, who

---

[60] Edward Hutchinson, *A Treatise Concerning the Covenant and Baptism*, p. 93.
[61] John Owen, *An Exposition of Hebrews 8:6-13*, p. 180.

was one and the same in both: For though Moses have the name of Mediatour."[62] Turretin goes in the same direction:

> Although Moses can in a measure be called a mediator in the Sinaitic Covenant [...] it does not follow that the covenant of which he is called the mediator was different in species form the Covenant of Grace, in which such a reconciliation is brought about. He was only a typical and external mediator, not a primary and true one from whom alone (his sponsion made and accepted by God) he had his whole power and efficacy to the reconciliation of sinners and their deliverance from the eternal curse and reception of heavenly life.[63]

John Owen opposed this idea that Christ was also the mediator of the Old Covenant:

> [...] this covenant, of which the Lord Christ is the mediator, is said to be a "better covenant." To that end it is supposed that there was another covenant, of which the Lord Christ was not the mediator. And in the following verses there are two covenants, a first and a latter, an old and a new, compared together[64].

The Presbyterians and the Baptists both believed that Christ's sacrifice was effective before being offered, however they saw the relationship of this effectiveness with the Old Covenant differently. Many paedobaptists considered that it was through the Old Covenant that Christ offered the benefits of his mediation to the believers that were under this covenant, while the Baptists affirmed the effectiveness of Christ's death from the revelation of the Covenant of Grace, but exclusively by virtue of the New Covenant. These two conceptions were very different; according to the paedobaptist conception, the work of Christ was communicated to believers both by the Old and New Covenants. For example,

---

[62] Thomas Blake, *Vindiciae Foederis,* p. 158. L'italique est de lui.
[63] Francis Turretin, *Institutes of Elenctic Theology,* vol. 2, p. 268.
[64] John Owen, *An Exposition of Hebrews 8:6-13,* p. 168.

Herman Witsius, in noting that the benefits of Christ's death existed before the arrival of the New Covenant, denied the New Testament exclusivity on these benefits. He writes:

> In the same base manner, they [Witsius designates in a general way those who saw a discontinuity between the Old and New Covenants] make the *writing the law on the heart*, a blessing peculiar to the New Testament: because Heb. viii. 10. it is said from Jer. xxxi. 34. "for this is the covenant that I will make with the house of Israel after those days, saith the Lord; I will put my laws into their mind, and write them in their hearts:" [...] If these words be taken as they lie, it follows, that the ancient believers, who lived before the times of the New Testament, did not receive the law of God, nor delight in it but forgot it. But that these things are most eminently false, appears from the example of David alone [...] How then is this a blessing peculiar to the New Testament, in which David claims an interest in so many words. [65]

Except for a few radical groups such as the Socinians, those who supported the New Testament exclusivity of Christ's mediation did not think claim that the benefits of Christ's death did not exist before New Testament times, but that they existed by virtue of it. Thus, the believers who lived before Christ were called and received the inheritance even if their transgressions had not yet been redeemed (Heb. 9.15). [66]

---

[65] Herman Witsius, *The Economy of the Covenants*, vol. 2, p. 335.

[66] On this point, certain paedobaptists had broken with Calvinist thought that was closer to the Baptist understanding. In commenting on Hebrews 8.10, Calvin writes the following: "But it may be asked, whether there was under the Law a sure and certain promise of salvation, whether the fathers had the gift of the Spirit, whether they enjoyed God's paternal favour through the remission of sins? Yes, it is evident that they worshipped God with a sincere heart and a pure conscience, and that they walked in his commandments, and this could not have been the case except they had been inwardly taught by the Spirit; and it is also evident, that whenever they thought of their sins, they were raised up by the assurance of a gratuitous pardon." Calvin continues by broaching the problem of the Old Testament prophecies that announced the forgiveness of sins as a thing to come,

Summary

In order to clarify our comparison of Presbyterian and Baptist federalism, here are two diagrams of their respective understandings. As a summary, we will explain these diagrams, and then we will end this chapter by examining some of the consequences of these two models.

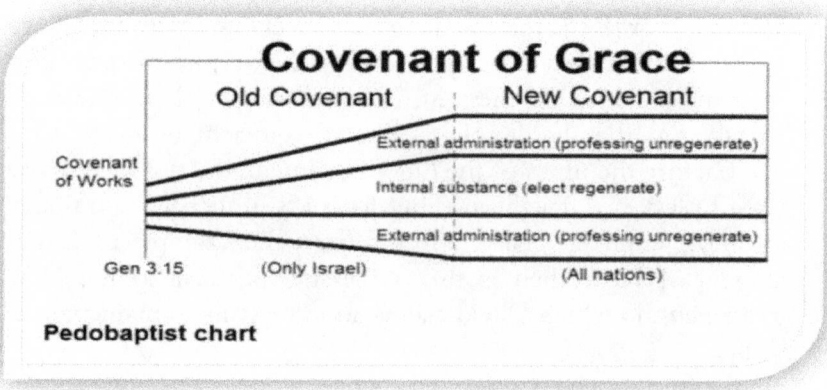

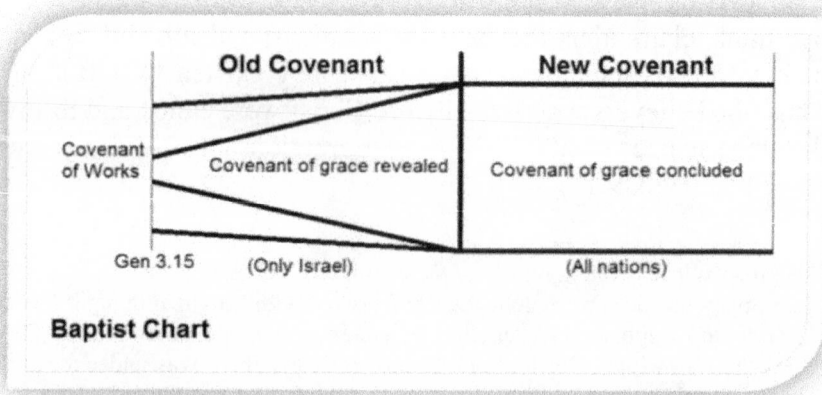

while salvation was already manifest. Then he responds to this question by affirming the effectiveness of the New Covenant before its establishment: "There is yet no reason why of should not have extended the grace of the new covenant to the fathers. This is the true solution of the question."

Let us first notice the harmony between the Westminster theology and that of the 1689. The first evidence of this harmony concerns the prelapsarian origin of the Covenant of Works and the postlapsarian beginning of the Covenant of Grace. Let us emphasize that both groups saw only one Church and one chosen people in both testaments. Thus, there is no duality between Israel and the Church as there was in Dispensationalism nor is there a replacement of Israel by the Church. The Church has existed since the beginning of the Covenant of Grace; the difference between the Old Testament and New Testament Churches consisted in the extent of the nations to which the Covenant of Grace was announced and not in the identity of the Church being different from one testament to another.[67]

---

[67] It would be impossible to exaggerate the importance of this point in order to avoid the failure to which the dialogue between reformed and dispensationalist theology has so often led. The Dispensationalists accused the reformed of creating a theology of replacement by giving the Church Israel's place, while Israel's place had to be permanent. Actually, historically, the reformed did not teach that the Church replaced Israel, but that the pagans joined Israel in the Covenant of Grace at the moment when the New Covenant replaced the Old Covenant. Thus, the promises of a perpetual covenant between Israel and God were not only maintained, but they were accomplished and extended to the pagans. It is, therefore, not the case of one people replacing another people, but the case of one covenant replacing another covenant when the promises revealed by the Covenant of Grace from Genesis 3.15 on were accomplished, when the Old Covenant ended and a large group made up of Jews and non-Jews entered into the New Covenant. One must refuse the opposition between Israel and the Church and rather emphasize the scope of the Covenant of Grace in the Old Testament (Israel) and the scope of the Covenant of Grace in the New Testament (every nation). The Gentiles do not replace Israel, but are added as inheritors of the blessings of Israel. The opposition that is found in the New Testament is between the Old and New Covenants and not between Israel and the Church, which is rather an artificial opposition coming from Dispensationalism.

We think that the Presbyterians have a harder time trying to demonstrate that Dispensationalism erroneously uses the discontinuity or opposition between the testaments since their own theology simply blurs this opposition, thereby denying, at least in the Dispensationalist view, the biblical affirmations of this discontinuity (Rom. 6.14; 2 Cor. 3; Jn. 1.17; Heb. 10.9). As for the Baptist approach, it allows for the vigorous assertion of the continuity of the Covenant of Grace and consequently, the continuity of only one Church in both testaments, all the while

A third similarity between both of these understandings is found in the progressive revelation of the Covenant of Grace. This notion is illustrated in both diagrams by the diagonal lines starting at Genesis 3.15.[68] We can note one last similarity: the Baptists and the Presbyterians recognized that under the Old Covenant there were those who were regenerated and those who were not. In the paedobaptist diagram, this notion is illustrated by a separation between those who were only under the external administration and those who were also under the internal substance of the Covenant of Grace. In the Baptist diagram, this notion of mixed nature is

---

affirming, in concert with the Bible and the Dispensationalists, a discontinuity between the Old and the New covenants.

The Dispensationalists, for their part, accentuated the discontinuity between the testaments to the point of separating Israel and the Church while giving a status as people of God to Israel, outside of the New Covenant while abolishing the Old Covenant (Israel's covenant). They then find themselves in a theological impasse: on one hand, they affirm the cessation of the Old Testament system during the era of the Church; on the other they must maintain the permanent validity of this system in order to justify the continuity of the existence of Israel as God's people. This contradiction is the main ambiguity of Dispensationalism: the end of the Old Testament at the same time as the maintaining of it. Their solution consists in separating Israel from the Church and temporarily putting the first aside during the time of the Church while preserving its initial status. This seems to us to be an artificial construction that does not take into account the definitive abolition of the Old Covenant without the promises that were made to Israel being abolished. These promises were accomplished, unbeknownst to the majority of the Jewish people, in Jesus Christ in the New Covenant and, while they first referred to Israel, they do not exclusively concern it, but extend themselves to all nations. Only the Baptist understanding seems to bring a solution that takes into account the biblical continuity and discontinuity.

[68] It should be noted that in both diagrams, the Old Covenant arrives in an equally progressive manner and covers the whole period of the Old Testament while certain paedobaptists made it start with Moses. Let us specify that these are simplified diagrams made to demonstrate the relationship between the Covenant of Grace and the two covenants called Old and New. In the next chapter, we will see the Old Covenant in greater detail; we will then specifically examine the Abrahamic covenant and the Sinaitic Covenant. Up until now we have spoken in general terms using the expression "Old Covenant" to cover the whole period of the Old Testament.

illustrated by the separation between the Old Covenant itself and the Covenant of Grace revealed under this covenant. The regenerated were both in the Covenant of Grace and under the Old Covenant and the non-regenerated were only under the Old Covenant. This notion of mixed nature corresponds to biblical data (cf. Rom. 9.6-8).

Secondly, let us examine the differences between the federalisms illustrated by these two diagrams. The first notable difference is the manifestation of the Covenant of Grace. On the paedobaptist side, the Covenant of Grace is everything that is after the fall. It is established as of Genesis 3.15 and concretized by two covenants: these two covenants are the Covenant of Grace. Consequently, these two covenants are simply seen as administrations and not as covenants in themselves; this is why these covenants are under the Covenant of Grace in the diagram and not the other way around. The dotted lines demonstrate that there is a progression in passing from the Old to the New Covenant, but there is no break. Therefore, we find a narrow continuity between these two administrations which is illustrated by the maintaining of the same terms of mixed nature from one covenant to the other.

On the Baptist side, it was considered that the Old Covenant was not a covenant of grace nor even an administration of it. Nevertheless, the Covenant of Grace was revealed progressively under the Old Covenant. The arrival of the New Covenant marks the full revelation of the Covenant of Grace which passes from the state of promise to the state of a covenant accomplished and sealed in blood. The Baptist diagram shows the Covenant of Grace coming to join the New Covenant without there being any distinction between them. The clear line between the Old and New Covenants illustrates the discontinuity between them and the end of the Old. With it ends the mixed nature amongst the people of God and the era of infancy (Gal. 4.3) characterized by the shadows of reality (Col. 2.17; Heb. 8.5; 10.1). This break in no way affects the continuity of the Covenant of Grace which is henceforth the only covenant through which God has a people and this covenant is the New Covenant.

4. A FEW COMPARISONS BETWEEN THESE TWO MODELS

Let us briefly compare some of the consequences implicit in these different models. Each one of these models rested on one fundamental distinction in the Covenant of Grace: the Presbyterians made a distinction between the substance and the administration of the Covenant of Grace, while the Baptists made a distinction between the revelation and the conclusion of the Covenant of Grace. These distinctions and these models had hermeneutical and theological consequences.

4.1. The hermeneutical comparisons

According to whether one adheres to the Presbyterian or to the Baptist model of the Covenant of Grace, the method of inter-pretation of the Bible which will ensue will be very different. Let us briefly examine how each model influences the biblical hermeneutic.

The Baptist federalists frequently faulted the paedobaptists for not letting Scripture define the covenants itself, and for altering them by defining them according to predefined parameters. The Baptists often insisted that the Old and New Covenants not be interpreted inside the global theological system of the Covenant of Grace, but rather that the Covenant of Grace be defined based on the biblical data regarding the Old and New Covenants. Fred Malone summarizes this crucial debate:

> Each covenant must be defined by revelation beyond the basic definition of a bond, pledge, oath, or promise. [...] In summary, classic paedobaptist covenantalists believe that the Covenant of Grace is the historical outworking of the Counsel of Redemption. Further, they believe that the Covenant of Grace of necessity includes a conditional curse and an organic element often included in some Old Testament covenants. This *a priori* assumption extends such elements into the New

Covenant by an erroneous inference against that which is expressly set down in Scripture.[69]

One of the fundamental rules of reformed hermeneutics consists in seeing Scripture as interpreting itself. The Baptists considered that paedobaptist federalism transgressed this rule by interpreting the biblical covenants based on a theological concept rather than on revelation. Nehemiah Coxe made this subtle reproach to the Presbyterians of his time in writing:

> Therefore the good and glory of any covenant that God makes with men, whether it be considered absolutely or in comparison with another covenant, is to be measured chiefly by its promises and terms. [...]

> Now it is evident from what has already been said, that all federal transactions of God with men flow only from his good pleasure and the counsel of his will. So, on that ground it is certainly to be concluded that our knowledge and understanding of them must wholly depend on divine revelation. [...]

> Yes, many great, learned, and good men have been divided in their judgments about some things of great importance to the faith and edification of the church though not absolutely necessary to her being. One error admitted about the nature of God's federal transactions with men strangely perplexes the

---

[69] Fred Malone, *The Baptism of Disciples Alone*, p. 59. The author takes on the hermeneutical principle at the basis of paedobaptist federalism "good a necessary inference" according to which one must deduce from the Old Testament the necessity for paedobaptism since it is not explicit in the New Testament. Dr Malone demonstrates that paedobaptism does not respect the hermeneutical rules that the Presbyterians caution and that this deduction is neither right nor necessary. Thomas Patient, in 1654, denounced this paedobaptist hermeneutic wherein deduction took priority over explicit revelation: "For any man to force a consequence that shall oppose itself against so solemn an ordinance cannot be of God. God cannot speak that which is contrary to Himself or to His own commands." Thomas Patient, *The Doctrine of Baptism, And the Distinction of the Covenants,* chapter 5.

whole system or body of divinity and entangles our
interpretation of innumerable texts of Scripture. [...] All this has
often occurred through the lack of a due and humble attention
to that revelation of truth which God has given us in the holy
Scriptures, and endeavoring to collect the mind of God from
there without a preconceived judgment, and a careful avoiding
of the undue mixture or confusion of things natural with those
that are purely of a federal nature.[70]

Was this accusation towards paedobaptists justified? Was it true
that they did not define the biblical covenants based on their
promises and respective terms but on pre-established theological
principles? In any case, it is undeniable that the paedobaptists
practised paedobaptism on the basis of a covenant where baptism
did not exist.[71] The only reason that explains this hermeneutic—
questionable to the Baptists—is the Presbyterian model of the
Covenant of Grace. This model had a major hermeneutical impact
since it led to the following logic: if the Covenant of Grace was
administered respectively by the Old and the New Covenants, they
were not really covenants, but only administrations of another
covenant which is progressively revealed through the Bible. This
logic explains the intertwining of the Old and New Testaments in
the paedobaptist hermeneutic. Consequently, there is no longer any
reason to define the terms and the ordinances of the New Covenant
based solely on New Testament data. It was to protect the
catechumens from this kind of hermeneutic that Edward Hutchinson
asked the following questions in his catechism:

---

[70] Nehemiah Coxe, *A Discourse of the Covenants*, p. 38, 40-41.
[71] Paedobaptist theologians generally had no problem admitting this: "Warfield
remarks, "The warrant for infant baptism is not to be sought in the New
Testament, but in the Old Testament." Louis Berkhof confirms this thought: "It
will be observed that all these statements are based on the commandment of God
to circumcise the children of the covenant, for in the last analysis that
commandment is the ground of infant baptism." Quoted by Samuel Waldron, *A
Modern Exposition of the 1689 Baptist Confession of Faith*, p. 350.

Quest. *Is not Baptism an Ordinance of the New Testament, and must it not be proved by a New-Testament Institution ?*
Answ. Yea.
Quest. *Where is your Institution then for Infant Baptism ?*
Answ. It is urged to be Gen. 17.7. I will be a God to thee and to thy Seed.
Quest. *Is there any thing concerning Baptism in this Scripture ?*
Answ. No, But we draw this Consequence, that as God promised to be God to Abraham and his Seed, so he will be a God to every Believer and his Seed[72].

In short, the main hermeneutic consequence of the *one covenant under two administrations* model is the levelling and amalgamation of both testaments. The paedobaptist approach not only did not use the New Testament to interpret the Old but did the exact opposite. David Kingdon writes: "Covenant theologians apply the wrong method of exegesis. Instead of recognizing that the New Testament fulfilment of the Covenant promises in Christ is far richer than the types of the Old Testament, they identify the two completely."[73] What is more, the paedobaptists defined the Old and the New covenants on the basis of predefined theological notions (for example: the Old and New covenants must have the same substance in order to preserve the unity of the Covenant of Grace) rather than on the basis of a biblical exegesis.

The Baptist understanding of the Covenant of Grace also had a great impact on hermeneutics. If the paedobaptist model left very little flexibility in the notion of discontinuity between the testaments, the Baptist model was easily able to bring together continuity and discontinuity in its federalism. Considering that the theological particularities of a group were always determined by the

[72] Edward Hutchinson, *Some Short Questions and Answers for the Younger Sort*, London, Printed for Francis Smith, 1676, (without pagination).
[73] David Kingdon, *Children of Abraham*, Sussex, Carey Publications, 1973, p. 6. Samuel Waldron declares what should be the correct hermeneutic method: "[T]he normative revelation for our understanding of the covenant of grace must remain the New Covenant." *A Modern Exposition of the 1689 Baptist Confession of Faith*, p. 110.

emphasis put on the continuity or discontinuity, the balance of the Baptist hermeneutic is particularly remarkable and allows for avoiding many pitfalls.

What permitted this flexibility and balance between the continuity and discontinuity was the distinction revealed/concluded in the Baptist model of the Covenant of Grace. There is a continuity because the Covenant of Grace was revealed starting in Genesis 3.15 until its full revelation in the New Testament, but there is also discontinuity because the Covenant of Grace was not concluded before the death and resurrection of Christ; the formal covenants that preceded this event had a different substance and were, therefore, abolished and replaced by the New Covenant. Among other things, the distinction revealed/concluded from the Covenant of Grace allowed for answering the Socinians of the time (or the dispensationalists of our time) who leaned on certain texts of the New Testament that seemed to teach that there was a time where salvation through faith in Christ did not exist. This text for example: "Before the coming of this faith, we were held in custody under the law, locked up until the faith that was to come would be revealed." (Gal. 3.23). The Baptist hermeneutic allowed the understanding that this text did not teach two parallel—or successive—methods of obtaining salvation. "Before the coming of this faith" refers to the period where the Gospel was at the state of a promise. When "the faith that was to come [was] revealed," that is, when the promise was accomplished, the law that led to it, meaning the Old Covenant, ceased. Therefore, the continuity of the Covenant of Grace is maintained at the same time that the discontinuity between the New Covenant (faith) and the Old Covenant (law) is affirmed.

Another text reads: "For the law was given through Moses; grace and truth came through Jesus Christ."(Jn.1.17). Was grace absent before the coming of Jesus Christ? (Truth would also have had to be absent.) Once again, the Baptist understanding of the Covenant of Grace allowed for the recognition of the discontinuity between

Moses and Jesus Christ without denying the efficacy of grace during Moses' time. [74] The same is true of other similar texts.

4.2. The theological comparisons

There can be no hermeneutic consequence without theological consequence. If federalism is the breaking point between the Presbyterians and the Baptists, it is in considering the theological consequences that we come to see where this mutual distancing leads. We have already glimpsed the theological particularities of each model during their presentation. We will now concentrate on three theological questions: (1) the way to enter into the Covenant of Grace; (2) the scope of grace in the Covenant of Grace and (3) the unconditional nature of the Covenant of Grace. These three questions could have, in themselves, been the subject of a position paper; we will only be able to treat them summarily.

4.2.1. The Way to Enter Into the Covenant of Grace

We have seen that Presbyterian federalism considers the Covenant of Grace on two levels: its spiritual substance and its natural administration. These are not two different covenants, but two realities within one covenant. This distinction allowed the Presbyterians to state that the Covenant of Grace contained both regenerated believers (internal spiritual substance) and people who professed the faith but were not regenerated (natural external administration). Paedobaptism requires this mixed nature since it justifies the inclusion of the posterity of believers in the covenant. By separating the internal substance from the external administration of the Covenant of Grace, one finds oneself with two categories of people in the same covenant: those who are saved, and those who are not. Consequently, for Presbyterians there were two

---

[74] It is also crucial to make the distinction between the law of Moses as a covenant and the law of Moses as commandments. The Covenant of the law as a legal term for the relationship of God with Israel was abolished, but the commandments of the law as rules of conduct are perpetuated by the New Testament.

ways to enter into the Covenant of Grace: one could enter when one was born or when one was born again.

The paedobaptists said that the Covenant of Grace was established with the Elect and that one entered into it through faith in Christ. Witsius writes: "The Covenant of Grace is a compact or agreement between God and the elect sinner."[75] Turretin made the same comment: "He entered into a twofold Covenant with men [...] By the latter [the Covenant of Grace], he promises to the believer safety in Christ and on account of Christ. [...] The latter was entered into with the elect in Christ after the fall."[76] However, the paedobaptists did not limit the Covenant of Grace exclusively to the elect; they also incorporated the posterity of believers into it. Consequently, repentance and faith were not seen as absolutely necessary in order to enter into the covenant; Ames writes:

> Faith and repentance no more constitute the covenant of God now than in the time of Abraham, who was the father of the faithful. Therefore, the lack of these ought not to prevent infants from being baptized any more than it prevented them from being circumcised then.[77]

Edward Hutchinson, a Baptist, revealed this particularity of Presbyterian federalism: that this understanding of the Covenant of Grace had to lead to the recognizing of two opposite ways (flesh vs. spirit) of entering into the covenant:

> Then it seems there are two wayes to come into the Covenant of Grace; one by being the Natural Child of a Believer; the other by Actual Faith. But this is ridiculous, for there is no being in the

---

[75] Herman Witsius, *The Economy of the Covenants*, vol. 1, p. 165.
[76] Francis Turretin, *Intitutes of Elenctic Theology,* vol. 2, p. 174.
[77] William Ames, *The Marrow of Theology*, p. 211.

Covenant of Grace, but by Election on Gods part; and actual Faith on Mans part.[78]

Of course, for the Baptists there was only one way to enter into the Covenant of Grace: through faith. This notion went along with their vision of the Covenant of Grace: revealed progressively before being concluded. Because they saw the Covenant of Grace as a promise (Ep. 2.12) announced then accomplished, the Baptists believed that faith was the only way to receive a promise. John Spilsbury writes:

> Thirdly, Who are the true approved Subjects of this Covenant, and they are onely such as beleeve; for God approves of none in covenant with him by his Word out of Christ, nor of any in Christ without faith. Nay, God denies his approving of any in fellowship or communion with him, that doe not beleeve [...]
>
> The fourth and last is this; Whether that all persons now under the Gospel, have not one and the same way of entrance into the foresaid Covenant?
>
> For answer to this, the holy Word of God must be Judge, and I finde the Gospel of Christ to approve of none in the Lords holy Covenant of Grace, but such as beleeve; neither any approved of, as to be in the way of life, but such as are in Christ by faith; and therefore no other way to come into the Covenant of Grace and salvation (as the Scriptures reveale) but only by Jesus Christ.[79]

For the Baptists, only faith constituted a valid entry into the Covenant of Grace. They did not consider the Covenant of Grace to be concluded simply with the elect, but with the converted elect. John Bunyan, in a discourse on law and grace, asked the following

---

[78] Edward Hutchinson, *Animadversions Upon a Late Book, Intituled, Infant Baptism From Heaven and not of Men, In Answer to Mr. Henry Danvers his Treatise of Baptism*, p. 28.
[79] John Spilsbury, *A Treatise Concerning the Lawfull Subject of Baptisme*, p. 9.

question: *"How are these brought into this everlasting Covenant of Grace?"*[80] In the pages that follow, he explains that it is by conversion that we enter into the Covenant of Grace and not by election. On this basis, the Baptists practised the baptism and ecclesiology of believers only. Inversely, it is because they saw two ways of entering into the Covenant of Grace that the paedobaptists practised the baptism and ecclesiology of believers and their posterity. This notion is clearly established in the Confession of Westminster. In chapter 25, the Church is looked at through two different realities: as an invisible entity and as a visible entity. These two notions correspond respectively to two ways of entering the Covenant of Grace and to the two levels of this covenant, i.e. its spiritual internal substance and its natural external administration.

> I. The catholic or universal Church, which is invisible, consists of the whole number of the elect, that have been, are, or shall be gathered into one, under Christ the Head thereof; and is the spouse, the body, the fullness of Him that filleth all in all.
> II. The visible Church, which is also catholic or universal under the Gospel (not confined to one nation, as before under the law), consists of all those throughout the world that profess the true religion; and of their children: and is the kingdom of the Lord Jesus Christ, the house and family of God, out of which there is no ordinary possibility of salvation.

Baptist ecclesiology, because it rested on a different federalism, rejected the Presbyterian notion of a visible Church made up of believers and their posterity. The Baptists kept paragraph 1 as is and rejected paragraph 2. Put differently, the Baptists supported the notion of an invisible Church made up of all of the elect, but for them, the Covenant of Grace was only included the elect who had been called; it did not have an external administration in which the non-elect were to be found; this is why they replaced paragraph 2, on the visible Church, with this one:

---

[80] John Bunyan, *The Doctrine of the Law and Grace Unfolded*, p. 541.

All persons throughout the world, professing the faith of the gospel, and obedience unto God by Christ according unto it, not destroying their own profession by any errors that undermine its foundation, or unholiness of conversation, are and may be called visible saints; and of such ought all particular congregations to be constituted.

Only authentic faith, according to the Baptists, allowed one to enter into the Covenant of Grace. Therefore, only those who had a credible profession of faith could make up the visible Church (which was not seen universally or nationally among Baptists, but locally).

This disagreement about the way to enter into the Covenant of Grace also applied to baptism: the paedobaptists baptized on the basis of new birth and natural birth, whereas the Baptists only practised baptism based on new birth. We believe that it was arbitrary on the part of paedobaptists to link baptism, not to the internal substance, but to the external administration of the Covenant of Grace since baptism symbolizes union in the death and resurrection of Christ (the ultimate spiritual substance of the Covenant of Grace). Henry Lawrence made a similar reproof: "Now we pretending to be Abraham's children by faith, not by carnal generation, cannot pretend to ordinances by carnal generation as the others did."[81] The paedobaptists did not purport to be in the Covenant of Grace as the natural descendants of Abraham, but as his spiritual descendants; however they practised a spiritual ordinance (baptism) on the basis of natural generation. A bit further, after having demonstrated that even the natural descendants of Abraham did not have the right to this ordinance on the basis of their natural heritage, but solely on the basis of their repentance (cf. Mat. 3.7-9), Lawrence concludes: "[…] if therefore the naturall seed of Abraham could not at all pretend to new Testament Ordinances a right by that title, much less the adopted seed by any such way of natural generation."[82]

---

[81] Henry Lawrence, *Of Baptism*, p. 93.
[82] *Ibid.*, p. 107.

Let us summarize. The paedobaptists would not have baptized
children without believing that they took part in the Covenant of
Grace. The Baptists would not have only baptized believers without
the conviction that they alone took part in the Covenant of Grace.
The paedobaptists believed that Christians and their posterity were
in the covenant because they saw two different levels to the
Covenant of Grace (internal and external), each of these levels
having its own entryway: one natural way and one spiritual way.
The Baptists believed that only the regenerated elect were in the
covenant because they only saw one level to the Covenant of Grace
into which one entered through faith alone.

4.2.2. The Range and Effectiveness of Grace in the Covenant of Grace

The second theological consequence of federalism is in connection
with the range and effectiveness of grace in the Covenant of Grace.
For the Baptists, being in the Covenant of Grace meant benefiting
from salvation by grace and all the privileges it entails. For the
Presbyterians, being in the Covenant of Grace did not necessarily
mean having salvation by grace or benefiting from all the privileges
it entails. There was, between these two groups, a fundamental
divergence with regards to the relationship between salvation itself
and the Covenant of Grace. The Baptists, in order to be able to
affirm that all the members of the Covenant of Grace were
regenerated elect, could not separate the covenant from salvation.
The paedobaptists, in order to be able to affirm that the Covenant of
Grace contained people who were saved and people who were lost,
had to separate the covenant from salvation. John Spilsbury
reproved the Presbyterians for this separation, as if one could exist
without the other:

> And if any shall say, that the Kingdome Christ speaks of, is
> meant the Kingdome of glory, and not of grace; and therefore
> though he excludes such out of the one, yet not out of the other.
> The answer is, that it is no where found in the Gospel, that any
> are excluded the Kingdome of glory, and yet are admitted into

the Kingdome of grace. The doore of grace in this sense, is no wider then [*sic*] the gate of glory by Gods appointment: and what men doe through ignorance, that alters not the truth of God, as Rom. 8.30.[83]

According to Spilsbury and his co-religionists, the members of the Covenant of Grace could not fail to end up in eternal glory. To enter into the Covenant of Grace was to enter into the gospel of glory, into the kingdom of Christ. Of course, the paedobaptist model of the Covenant of Grace saw things differently. By separating the substance from its administrations, they separated salvation from its visible manifestation, i.e. the Church since it itself was not saved; only the elect were saved. Thus, one could not say that Christ had saved his Church (cf. Ep. 5.23-27). According to this conception, Christ would have only saved part of his Church.[84] All the particularities of this federalism are present in this paragraph where John Ball explains the two categories of people who are part of the Covenant of Grace, that is, part of the Church:

> And these be of two sorts; for God doth make his Covenant with some externally, calling them by his Word, and sealing them by his Sacraments, and they by profession of faith and receiving of the Sacraments oblige themselves to the condition required: and thus all members of the visible Church be in Covenant. With others God doth make his Covenant effectually, writing his Law in their hearts by his holy Spirit, and they freely and from the heart give up themselves unto the Lord, in all things to be ruled and guided by him. And thus God hath contracted Covenant with the faithfull only. The first sort is the

---

[83] John Spilsbury, *A Treatise Concerning the Lawfull Subject of Baptisme*, p. 30

[84] This is exactly what Herman Witisus affirms while taking care to say that Christ did not die for the visible Church, but for the elect only, in other words, only part of the Church: "When Paul said, that Christ purchased his church with his own blood, Acts xx. 28, he more distinctly explains in his epistle to the Ephesians, v. 25. What he means by the church, which Christ loved and gave himself for, namely, the spouse of Christ, whom alone he loves with a conjugal affection [...] But that love of Christ [...] belongs to elect believers only." *The Economy of the Covenants*, vol. 1, p. 266.

people of God outwardly or openly, having all things externall and pertaining to the outward administration. The second are the people of God inward or in secret, whom certainly and distinctly the Lord only knoweth[85].

Witsius formulated this same doctrine by distinguishing between the Covenant of Grace and the two testaments; salvation would belong to the essence of the Covenant of Grace, but not to its administrations: "The promise of the common salvation which is in Christ, whether formerly made to the fathers, or to us at this day, does not belong to the Old and New Testaments, but absolutely to the testament or Covenant of Grace."[86] All the Presbyterians separated salvation and the Covenant of Grace on the basis of the internal spiritual substance/natural external administration distinction; this is still the case today.

This understanding raised an important question: what benefit was there for those who were in the Covenant of Grace who did not benefit from salvation? Generally, the paedobaptists indicated that the privileges of the non-saved members of the Covenant of Grace were the blessings of belonging to the visible Church. For example, Samuel Petto writes: "*As to advantages, there are many as a Covenant state is a state of greater nearness unto God then* [sic] *others are in."*[87] Thomas Blake admitted that such a state did not operate any internal change in man: "That Covenant between God and man [...] is a Covenant onely visibly entered, and doth not require any inward reall change, or work upon the soul to the being of it."[88] A little farther on, he affirms that such a state was nonetheless a blessing: "Men brought into a visible Church-state, are brought into a marvelous light."[89] What remained fundamental was that it was conceived that all the blessings of the Covenant of Grace

---

[85] John Ball, *A Treatise of the Covenant of Grace*, p. 202-3.
[86] Herman Witsius, *The Economy of the Covenants*, vol. 1, p. 308.
[87] Samuel Petto, *Infant Baptism of Christ's Appointment*, London, Printed for Edward Giles, 1687, p. 66. The italics are the author's.
[88] Thomas Blake, *Vindiciae Foederis*, p. 193.
[89] *Ibid.*, p. 203.

came directly from the mediation of Christ. It was therefore possible to benefit from the mediation of Christ without being saved, to partially benefit from the effects of his redemption. John Ball writes:

> Others proper to the members of the visible Church and common to them, as to be called by the word, injoy the Ordinances of grace, live under the Covenant, partake of some graces that come from Christ, which through their fault be not saving: *and in this sence Christ died for all that be under the Covenant.*[90]

This manner of limiting Christ's mediation within the Covenant of Grace appears highly problematic to us. The Presbyterians perceived the scope and efficacy of the Covenant of Grace in a restrained way because they had to maintain an essential characteristic of their ecclesiology: the mixed nature of the people of the covenant. They therefore had to understand the mediation of Christ in such a way as to be able to include the "unconverted" amongst his people. Thus, the efficacy of the grace of salvation could not reach out endlessly to the people of the Covenant even if the people had Christ as a mediator. In order to justify the mixed nature of the Church, the paedobaptists had to restrain the efficacy of grace to within the covenant. As a result, the *one covenant under two administrations* model had a direct consequence on the doctrine of expiation.

The Baptists compared this restrained efficacy of the death of Christ to a kind of limited Arminianism. This Arminianism extended the reach of the death of Christ to all human beings, but limited its efficacy to believers. Presbyterian federalism extended the reach of the death of Christ to all the members of the covenant, but limited its salvific efficacy to the elect. Consequently, Presbyterian federalism

---

[90] John Ball, *A Treatise of the Covenant of Grace*, p. 206. Italics added. However Herman Witsius denied that Christ had given himself for the visible Church in a general way; he writes: "He has engaged and satisfied for those, and those only, who are actually saved from their sins." *The Economy of the Covenants*, vol. 1, p.255-6 (cf. also p. 265, XXII). Witsius understood the danger of extending Christ's mediation to the unsaved of the visible church; unfortunately, he does not explain how they benefited from the grace of the Covenant of Grace.

was comparable to Arminianism, but limited to the Covenant of Grace. Fred Malone shares this opinion when he writes:

> Another problem with the paedobaptist position that all physical infants of believers are in the New Covenant is that it does violation to the doctrine of particular redemption. Every New Covenant member has Jesus Christ as his effectual Mediator (Matthew 1:21). As Ridderbos says: "God's people are those for whom Christ sheds his blood of the covenant. They share in the remission of sins brought about by him and in the unbreakable communion with God in the New Covenant that he has made possible." To call unregenerate infants "God's people" and members of the New Covenant for "whom Christ sheds his blood of the covenant" violates particular redemption simply because no one can be in the New Covenant without the effectual mediatorial sacrifice that establishes the covenant with every member.[91]

Well before Dr. Malone, Dr. Owen had taken on this fallacy of Presbyterian federalism in his famous *The Death of Death in the Death of Christ*, where he writes the following against the Arminian conception of redemption:

> The first argument may be taken from the nature of the covenant of grace, which was established, ratified, and confirmed in and by the death of Christ; that was the testament whereof he was the testator, which was ratified in his death, and whence his blood is called "The blood of the new testament," Matt. xxvi. 28. Neither can any effects thereof be extended beyond the compass of this covenant. But now this covenant was not made universally with all, but particularly only with some, and therefore those alone were intended in the benefits of the death of Christ. [...]

> And this is the main difference between the Old Covenant of works and the new one of grace, that in that the Lord did only require the fulfilling of the condition prescribed, but in this he

---

[91] Fred Malone, *The Baptism of Disciples Alone*, p. 95-96.

promiseth to effect it in them himself with whom the covenant is made. And without this spiritual efficacy, the truth is, the New Covenant would be as weak and unprofitable, for the end of a covenant (the bringing of us and binding of us to God), as the old. [...] This, then, is one main difference of these two covenants, - that the Lord did in the old only require the condition; now, in the new, he will also effect it in all the federates, to whom this covenant is extended. And if the Lord should only exact the obedience required in the covenant of us, and not work and effect it also in us, the New Covenant would be a show to increase our misery, and not a serious imparting and communicating of grace and mercy. If, then, this be the nature of the new testament, -as appears from the very words of it, and might abundantly be proved, be wrought and accomplished in all that are taken into covenant, then no more are in this covenant than in whom those conditions of it are effected.[92]

Owen repeats the same theology in his exposition of the Epistle to the Hebrews:

The New Covenant is made with them alone who effectually and eventually are made partakers of the grace of it. "This is the covenant that I will make with them... I will be merciful to their unrighteousness," etc. Those with whom the Old Covenant was made were all of them actual partakers of the benefits of it; and if they are not so with whom the new is made, it comes short of the old in efficacy, and may be utterly frustrated. Neither does the indefinite proposal of the terms of the covenant prove that the covenant is made with them, or any of them, who enjoy not the benefits of it. *Indeed this is the excellence of this covenant, and so it is here declared, that it does effectually communicate all the grace and mercy contained in it to all and every one with whom it is made; with whomsoever it is made, his sins are pardoned.*[93]

---

[92] John Owen, "The Death of Death in the Death of Christ." *The Works of John Owen,* volume 10, Carlisle, The Banner of Truth Trust, 1968 (1647), p. 236-237.

[93] John Owen, *An Exposition of Hebrews 8:6-13*, p. 303 (italics added).

In reading these lines, one asks oneself on what basis Owen practised child baptism. First, it is evident that he made a radical distinction between the Old and New Covenants and their respective natures. Owen considered that the Old Covenant was effective for all of its members, without them all being saved, since, as he explicitly states elsewhere, this covenant did not give salvation. We also see that the prince of Puritans rejected the mixed nature of the Covenant of Grace because he could not conceive that Christ would have died for members of the covenant that were not saved. According to Owen's conception, one can partially benefit from Christ's death; it is fully effective for the totality of the members of the covenant. If someone does not benefit from the salvific grace of the Covenant of Grace, he is simply not a part of the covenant.

The Baptists had the same understanding. The reach of the grace within the Covenant of Grace had to extend itself to all the members. The son of Benjamin Coxe writes:

> The sum of all gospel blessings is comprised in this promise [God's promise to Abraham]. Therefore it will follow that the proper heirs of this blessing of Abraham have a right (not only in some, but) in all the promises of the New Covenant. This is true not in a limited sense, suspended on uncertain conditions, but in a full sense and secured by the infinite grace, wisdom, power, and faithfulness of God. Accordingly, they are in time made good to them all. And this will be more manifest if we consider that all the blessings of this covenant redound on believers by means of their union and communion with the Lord Jesus Christ, who is both the Head and Root of the New Covenant, and the Fountain from which all its blessings are derived to us. *Since these blessings were entirely purchased by him, so are they entirely applied to all that are in him and to none other.*
>
> *Therefore, I conceive the limiting of a New Covenant interest to the grand of an external and temporary privilege only, to be utterly inconsistent with the promises of the covenant itself* (such as these: Isaiah 54:13; 59:21; Jeremiah 31:33, 34; Ezekiel 36:26, 27 with Hebrews 8 and many others of like import). Neither will these texts admit of another

notion lately insisted on for the commendation of paedobaptism.[94]

From a Baptist point of view, a Church of mixed nature, where some benefited from salvation and others from partial blessings, altered the spiritual nature of the covenant between Christ and His Church and profaned the nature and the efficacy of the work of Christ. Spilsbury writes: "It is a high contempt and injury to Christ, as he is the husband of the Church his holy Spouse, to force upon him an naturall wife."[95]

Regarding the apostates, whom the paedobaptists saw as transgressors of the covenant, the Baptists considered that they had simply never been members of the covenant (cf 1Jn. 2.19).

4.2.3. The unconditional nature of the Covenant of Grace

These two different conceptions of the Covenant of Grace had a direct impact on the way of seeing the conditional or unconditional nature of the Covenant of Grace.[96] By limiting the Covenant of Grace to only the regenerate elect, the Baptists could easily affirm that it was absolutely unconditional.

On the Presbyterian side, several also stated the unconditional nature of the Covenant of Grace.[97] However, how could a covenant from which one could fall be unconditional? This was an important paradox in Presbyterian federalism. For example, Peter Bulkeley affirmed that one could sin against the Covenant of Grace is such a way as to transgress it and render it invalid.[98] However, he later

---

[94] Nehemiah Coxe, *A Discourse of the Covenants*, p. 81. Italics added.

[95] John Spilsbury, *A Treatise Concerning the Lawfull Subject of Baptisme*, p. 25

[96] Cf, Keach, *The Display of Glorious Grace*, p. 173; *The Everlasting Covenant*, p. 34. Patient, *The Doctrine of Baptism, And the Distinction of the Covenants*, chapters 7 and 9. Owen, *An Exposition of Hebrews 8:6-13*, p. 259ss. Bunyan, *The Doctrine of the Law and Grace Unfolded*, p. 524, 534.

[97] Cf. Francis Turretin, *Institutes of Elenctic Theology*, vol. 2, p. 184ff. It is the third question of his twelfth subject (the Covenant of grace): "Is the covenant of grace conditional and what are its conditions?".

[98] Peter Bulkeley, *The Gospel Covenant; or The Covenant of Grace Opened*, p. 95.

writes: "One that is under the covenant of works, may get from under that covenant, and may come to be under the covenant of grace, but he that is once under the covenant of grace, can never be brought back under the covenant of works any more."[99] Consequently, Presbyterian federalism had a fundamental difficulty in seeing the Covenant of Grace as being absolutely unconditional and was confronted with an implacable antinomy.[100]

CONCLUSION

In this chapter we have seen two different understandings of the Covenant of Grace and of its relationship to the Old and New Covenants. The paedobaptist model perceived the beginning of the Covenant of Grace immediately right after the fall and placed this covenant under two successive administrations called the Old and New Covenants. By distinguishing between the covenant (substance) and its administrations (circumstance), Presbyterians established a foundation which was essential to them: they could maintain natural heirs and spiritual heirs within the same covenant, the first having part in the administration only and the second having part in both the administration and the substance of the Covenant of Grace. Paedobaptist federalism and ecclesiology were based on this distinction.

The Baptist understanding rested on another fundamental distinction: one between the phase where the Covenant of Grace was revealed and the phase where it was concluded. The revealed phase corresponded to the period preceding the death of Christ and the concluded phase corresponded to the time that followed. Therefore,

---

[99] *Ibid.*, p. 99-100.

[100] We will content ourselves to simply raise the problem without examining it further since it was treated in depth by Jeffrey Johnson who dedicates chapters 7, 8 and 9 of *The Fatal Flaw of the Theology Behind Infant Baptism*. Johnson reviews the six alternatives left to the paedobaptists with regards to this problem. He demonstrates that biblical orthodoxy is incompatible with Presbyterian federalism and, that the latter, if it wants to be consistent with itself, must sacrifice orthodoxy by removing the unconditional nature of grace.

Baptists considered that no other covenant, besides the New Covenant, was the Covenant of Grace. They still recognized that the Covenant of Grace had been revealed under all the covenants since the fall, but distinguished between the actual substance of these covenants and the Covenant of Grace itself.

These two federalisms were at the root of all the divergences between the Presbyterians and the Baptists of the seventeenth century. Their understandings of the Covenant of Grace led them toward different hermeneutics and theological notions. In the last part of this work, we will see how their respective understandings of the Covenant of Grace determined the rest of their federalism. In other words, we will see how the Presbyterian and Baptists models determined the perception of the Old and New Covenants of both of these groups.

Chapter 3
The Old Covenant

1. WHAT DOES THE EXPRESSION "OLD COVENANT" MEAN?

Up to this point, we have frequently used the expression "Old Covenant" without specifying what it designates. The Scriptures use this expression to designate the covenant concluded between God and Israel upon the exodus from Egypt, the covenant of which Moses was the mediator (compare Jer. 31.31-32 and Heb. 8.8-13)[1]. For most seventeenth-century federalists, the expression "Old Covenant" referred to the Mosaic Covenant;[2] however, it also referred to more than that. According to them, the Old Covenant included the whole Old Testament period, that is, from the fall until the establishment of the New Covenant. Federal theology saw the Old Covenant as being cumulative.

1.1. The Cumulative aspect of the Old Covenant

It is easy to determine the end of the Old Covenant since it was abolished when it was replaced by the New Covenant (cf. Heb. 7.11-19). It is, however, more difficult to determine the beginning of the Old Covenant. There is no doubt that the covenant concluded in the Sinai desert determined the Old Covenant, but did it initiate it? Before the Sinaitic Covenant, did the Old Covenant exist? We believe that the establishment of the Old Covenant started before the arrival of the Sinaitic Covenant. This covenant was concluded on the basis of a covenant between Abraham and God (cf. Ex. 2.24; 3.15-

---

[1] The New Testament also refers to this covenant without calling it the Old Covenant: 2 Cor. 3; Gal. 3-4.

[2] Some use the expression "Sinaitic Covenant"; we will use both interchangeably.

16; 6.4-8). Several times, the New Testament presents the covenant between God and Israel (the Old Covenant) rooted both in the covenant with the patriarchs and in the Mosaic Covenant. Jesus and Paul join the circumcision given to Abraham and the law given to Moses in an indissociable way (Jn. 7.22-23; Gal. 5.3). Steven starts his overview of the Old Covenant with Abraham and he also includes the Mosaic and Davidic Covenants in this overview (Ac. 7). The apostles associate circumcision with the burden of the Law of Moses (Ac. 15.5, 10-11). The Epistle to the Hebrews affirms that Christ paid for the sins committed under the first covenant (Heb. 9.15), namely all the sins committed before the death of Christ since the fall. The first covenant, therefore, covered the entire period going from the fall to the establishment of the New Covenant.[3]

Reformed theologians did not see "the covenants of the promise" (Ep. 2.12) as being several covenants independent of one another, but as cumulative covenants. The Presbyterians and the Baptists were in agreement on this point.[4] Herman Witsius writes: "We begin the economy of the Old Testament immediately upon the fall, and the first promise of grace, and end it in Christ."[5] On the Baptist side of things, Nehemiah Coxe writes:

---

[3] This does not mean that the first covenant (the Old Covenant) would have been uniform since the beginning. The reformed perceived several phases of development which led to the full establishment of the Old Covenant: from Adam to Noah, from Noah to Abraham, from Abraham to Moses, from Exodus to Canaan, etc. Cf. Herman Witsius, *The Economy of the Covenants*, vol. 1, p. 313ff. It should also be noted that the animal sacrifices, which were at the basis of the Old Covenant (Heb. 7.11), started well before the Levitical priesthood. Sacrifices are present as of Genesis (Gn. 3.21; 4.4; 8.20; 22.13; 46.1) and the Levitical priesthood represents their continuity.

[4] It seems that this understanding was the norm of Calvinism at this time. This notion goes back to Calvin himself, Peter Lillback writes: "Calvin explains the relationship of Abraham and Moses in terms of the single covenant of God in the progress of redemptive history." Cf. "Calvins's Interpretation of the History of Salvation," *Theological Guide to Calvin's Institutes*, Phillipsburg, P&R, 2008, p. 187.

[5] Herman Witsius, *The Economy of the Covenants*, vol. 1, p. 308. See also John Ball, *A Treatise of the Covenant of Grace*, p. 36.

[W]e must further observe that this covenant of circumcision was the foundation on which the church-state of Israel after the flesh was built.

I do not say that their church-state was exactly and completely formed by this ordinance alone. But I mean that in the covenant of circumcision were contained the first rudiments of the one in the wilderness, and the latter was the filling up and completing of the former. It was made with them in pursuance of it and for the full accomplishment of the promises now made to Abraham.[6]

Thomas Patient is even more explicit: "But it is clear to me that in substance, the same covenant of ceremonial obedience which was given to Moses when the people came out of Egypt, the same was given to Adam's generation."[7]

1.2. A Difficulty for the paedobaptists

This cumulative notion of the Old Covenant could harmonize both with the Presbyterian and Baptist understandings of the Covenant of Grace. However, if one considered the Sinaitic Covenant as a covenant of works (i.e. conditional), it became impossible to consider the Old Covenant as a cumulative administration of the Covenant of Grace since there would have been an incompatibility between the unconditional nature of the Covenant of Grace and the conditional nature of the Sinaitic Covenant. Of course, most Presbyterians did not have this difficulty since they did not see the Sinaitic Covenant as a covenant of works, but as a covenant of grace. On the other hand, some paedobaptists, in accordance with the Baptists, saw the Sinaitic Covenant as a conditional covenant. Two alternatives were available to the paedobaptists: denying the conditional aspect of the Mosaic Covenant in order to associate it

---

[6] Nehemiah Coxe, *A Discourse of the Covenants*, p. 99.
[7] Thomas Patient, *The Doctrine of Baptism, And the Distinction of the Covenants*, beginning of Chapter 10.

with the Covenant of Grace or placing the Mosaic Covenant aside and isolating it from the Covenant of Grace.[8]

These approaches were both aimed at maintaining the *one Covenant of Grace under two administrations* paradigm. The federalism of that of 1689 (*the Covenant of Grace revealed then concluded*) avoided this difficulty. Actually, the Baptists considered the Sinaitic Covenant as a covenant of works that could exist in parallel and simultaneously with the Covenant of Grace without compromising it.

On the Presbyterian side, none of the offered alternatives was without difficulty. In the case where one denied the conditionality of the Mosaic Covenant in order to integrate it into the Covenant of Grace, it was necessary to explain several passages of the Bible that, at the very least, seemed to suggest that the Mosaic Covenant was conditional and was not a covenant of grace. In the case where one admitted the conditionality of the Mosaic Covenant, it was necessary to find a way to affirm the unity of the Covenant of Grace in the Old Testament without compromising the unconditional nature of this covenant. This way consisted in hermeneutically separating the Abrahamic Covenant from the Mosaic Covenant; the first being the Covenant of Grace and the second a covenant of works. However, how does one explain the organic continuity that all saw, between Abraham and Moses? Let us examine each of these solutions in turn.

1.2.1. Solution 1: the Mosaic Covenant was unconditional

The Holy Scriptures present two ways of obtaining the divine blessing: in a conditional way or in an unconditional way. With the

---

[8] A third alternative was foreseeable and consisted simply in considering the Covenant of Grace as being conditional (or partially conditional). This tendency eventually led the paedobaptists toward the controversy of the *Federal Vision* and the NPP, cf. Jeffrey D. Johnson, *The Fatal Flaw of the Theology Behind Infant Baptism*, chapters 8 and 9.

first is associated obedience to the law, and with the second is associated faith. Regarding the conditional blessing obtained through obedience to the law we read: "Keep my decrees and laws, for the person who obeys them will live by them. I am the Lord." (Lev. 18.5). With regards to the unconditional blessing obtained through faith we read: "[...] but the righteous person will live by his faithfulness" (Hab. 2.4). Man can live (i.e. obtain life) by the law (Rom. 10.5), or he can live by faith (Rom. 1.17). These two ways are contrary to one another and are mutually exclusive. The apostle Paul writes:

> [10] For all who rely on the works of the law are under a curse, as it is written: "Cursed is everyone who does not continue to do everything written in the Book of the Law." [11]Clearly no one who relies on the law is justified before God, because "the righteous will live by faith." [12]The law is not based on faith; on the contrary, it says, "The person who does these things will live by them." (Gal. 3:10-12)

In federal theology, a covenant or promised inheritance which was conditional on the obedience of federates was considered to be a covenant of works. A covenant wherein the promised inheritance was given unconditionally to all federates was considered to be a covenant of grace. Thus, the obedience of federates was seen either as the cause, or as the consequence of the blessing received through the covenant. John Owen explains how obedience works within a covenant of grace and within a covenant of works:

> The promises of the covenant of grace are better than those of any other covenant, as for many other reasons, so especially because the grace of them prevents any condition or qualification on our part. I do not say the covenant of grace is absolutely without conditions, if by conditions we intend the duties of obedience which God requires of us in and by virtue of that covenant; but this I say, the principal promises of it are not in the first place remunerative of our obedience in the covenant, but efficaciously assumptive of us into covenant, and establishing or confirming in the covenant. The covenant of

works had its promises, but they were all remunerative, respecting an antecedent obedience in us; (so were all those which were peculiar to the covenant of Sinai). They were, indeed, also of grace, in that the reward did infinitely exceed the merit of our obedience; but yet they all supposed it, and the subject of them was formally reward only. In the covenant of grace it is not so; for several of the promises of it are the means of our being taken into covenant, of our entering into covenant with God. The first covenant absolutely was established on promises, in that when men were actually taken into it, they were encouraged to obedience by the promises of a future reward. But those promises, namely, of the pardon of sin and writing of the law in our hearts, on which the apostle expressly insists as the peculiar promises of this covenant, do take place and are effectual antecedently to our covenant obedience. For although faith be required in order of nature antecedently to our actual receiving of the pardon of sin, yet is that faith itself produced in us by the grace of the promise, and so its precedence to pardon respects only the order that God had appointed in the communication of the benefits of the covenant, and intends not that the pardon of sin is the reward of our faith.[9]

Most covenant theologians of the seventeenth century supported this understanding. However, many applied the notion of obedience of the Covenant of Grace to the Mosaic Covenant. Consequently, the obedience required by the Law of Moses was not seen as the condition for inheriting the blessing, but as the fruit of the unconditional blessing offered by this covenant. For example, John Ball used passages such as Deuteronomy 9.4-5 to demonstrate that the inheritance promised to Israel was not conditional on its obedience[10] and he explains the conditional passages in the following way:

---

[9] John Owen, *An Exposition of Hebrews 8:6-13*, p. 178-79.

[10] Those who saw the Sinaitic Covenant as a covenant of works, saw this kind of passage as an extraordinary manifestation of the grace of God, merciful even under a covenant of works, therefore infinitely merciful under a covenant of grace.

True it is the promises runne upon this condition, «*If ye obey my voice and doe my Commandements.* But conditions are of two sorts, antecedent or consequent. Antecedent, when the condition is the cause of the thing promised or given […] Consequent, when the condition is annexed to the promise as a qualification in the Subject, or an adjunct, that must attend the thing promised. And in this latter sence, obedience to the Commandments, was a condition of the promise; not a cause why the thing promised was vouchsafed, but a qualification in the subject capable, or a consequence of such great mercy freely conferred.[11]

For Ball, there was no difference between the goal of the obedience required by Jesus Christ and the goal of the obedience required by Moses. In no case did he see obedience as a conditional cause of the promises, but only as an effect of these promises. Thomas Blake affirmed that the Old and New Covenants offered and required exactly the same thing. "These Covenants have both one and the same conditions [sic] on Gods part, remission of sins and everlasting happinesse […] they are the same on mans part, Faith and Repentance."[12] Further on, he explains that the conditions of faith functioned as a covenant of works for those who did not have faith, but as a covenant of grace for believers.[13] Blake considered that the Ten Commandments, within the Sinaitic Covenant, were exactly the same as the law written in the heart under the New Covenant because he saw the Sinaitic Covenant as a covenant of grace. He writes:

This Covenant delivered by Moses to the people of Israel, was a covenant of grace, the same in substance with this under which we live in Gospel-times. This is so largely proved to my hand by Master Ball in his Treatise of the Covenant, page 102, 103, 104.[14]

---

[11] John Ball, *A Treatise of the Covenant of Grace*, p. 132-33.
[12] Thomas Blake, *Vindiciae Foederis,* p. 158-59.
[13] *Ibid.*, p. 172
[14] *Ibid.*, p. 166.

Since Blake relies entirely on the work of John Ball to affirm that the Mosaic Covenant was unconditional, let us examine three pieces of evidence that he gives.[15] His first piece consists in saying that in making the covenant with Israel, God was extending grace. Consequently, this covenant was not conditional, but unconditional, it was not due, but given freely. However, all confessions recognized that "The distance between God and the creature is so great, that [...] they could never have attained the reward of life but by some voluntary condescension on God's part, which he hath been pleased to express by way of covenant."[16] This included the initial Covenant of Works. All covenants between God and man, including a conditional covenant, is an act of goodwill, a favour, but not necessarily a covenant of grace.

Secondly, Ball examines the introduction of the Decalogue in Chapter 19 of the Book of Exodus and concludes that grace preceded the commandments since God delivered Israel before giving them his law. The obedience required by the commandments would, therefore, not be anterior and conditional, but ulterior and consequent to the blessing offered in this covenant. There is no doubt that the deliverance from Egypt was unconditional, but it was not by virtue of this deliverance nor during its time that God made a covenant with Israel. God had delivered Israel by grace beforehand, but later established a conditional covenant with her.

At the same time, where Ball specifically sees a covenant of grace, in the introduction of the Mosaic Covenant, is in this promise: "I will be your God and you will be my people." He writes:

> The Covenant of Grace is expressed in these words, *I will be thy God and thou shalt be my people:* Wherein God promiseth to be favourable to the iniquity of his servants, and to remember their

---

[15] John Ball, *A Treatise of the Covenant of Grace*, p. 102-110. Ball gives eight pieces of evidence in total, but they are intertwined and can be summarized in three points. We will briefly explain why we think that Ball's evidence is flawed and we will demonstrate it in the rest of this dissertation.

[16] *La Confession de foi baptiste de Londres de 1689*, 7.1.

sins no more: and to blesse them with all spirituall blessings in heavenly things.[17]

Ball was not the only one to see that to have God as one's God necessarily meant to be in the Covenant of Grace; Herman Witsius writes: "That expression, *to be God to any*, in its full import, includes life eternal. For when God becomes the sinner's God, he then becomes to him, what he is to himself."[18] We believe that this deduction is mistaken for two reasons. Firstly because Scripture sets out a way to have God as one's God other than by salvation through grace. With regards to this, Nehemiah Coxe writes the following:

> It is evident that this promise, "I will be their God," and the earlier one found in Genesis 17:7 give a general assurance of some good to the people in covenant. But it should not be supposed that they are promises of some particular good or blessing that is of a higher nature than is comprehended in any other promises of the covenant. *For the true import of this general promise is "that God has engaged himself and all the properties of his nature for the exact fulfilling of all the promises of the covenant now made with them, according to the true character and conditions of the said covenant."* All the divine perfections are laid in as pledges that the promises will not fail on God's part since they will be all exerted, as the need requires, for the good and advantage of this people in fulfilling the promises given to them. But still God's communications to them and acts for them, both in

---

[17] John Ball, *A Treatise of the Covenant of Grace*, p. 104.
[18] Herman Witsius, *The Economy of the Covenants*, vol. 1, p. 293. John Calvin had the same understanding: "The covenant which God always made with his servants was this, "I will walk among you, and will be your God, and ye shall be my people," (Lev. 26:12). These words, even as the prophets are wont to expound them, comprehend life and salvation, and the whole sum of blessedness. For David repeatedly declares, and with good reason, "Happy is that people whose God is the Lord." "Blessed is the nation whose God is the Lord; and the people whom he has chosen for his own inheritance" (Psalm 144:15; 33:12); and this not merely in respect of earthly happiness, but because he rescues from death, constantly preserves, and, with eternal mercy, visits those whom he has adopted for his people." *Institution*, II, X, 8.

regard to the blessings he will bestow and the terms and conditions on which they will be bestowed, are limited by the covenant he has made with them and the nature and extent of the promises of it.[19]

In other words, what having God as one's God implies must be determined based on the terms of the covenant by which God commits to being God for his people. As the Creator, is not God the God of all men (Ps. 24.1; Mal 2.10; Mt 5.45; 1 Tim. 4.10; 2 Pet. 2.1)? As the redeemer of Israel, he was the God of all people without all people necessarily benefiting from the grace of salvation (Rom. 9.6-8); nevertheless, this same people is often called the people of God (Deut. 27.9; 2 Rom. 9.6; Ps. 50.7). By committing to being the God of Israel, the Lord was promising her superiority over other nations, protection, the possession of Canaan, the blessing of her land... (cf. Deut. 28.1-14). Only the terms of the covenant concluded in the Sinai desert can tell us to what God was committing by promising to be the God of Israel.

Secondly, as Coxe indicates, one must take into account the nature of this promise when it is found in one covenant or in another: is it a conditional or an unconditional promise? A simple comparison of this same promise in the context of the Sinaitic Covenant and in that of the New Covenant is very revealing. Under the Old Covenant God says: "Now *if* you obey me fully and keep my covenant, then out of all nations you will be my treasured possession. Although the whole earth is mine, you will be for me a kingdom of priests and a holy nation." (Ex. 19.5-6, italics added). Having God according to the terms defined by the Old Covenant was conditional on Israel's obedience.[20] Under the New Covenant

---

[19] Nehemiah Coxe, *A Discourse of the Covenants*, p. 111. Italics added.

[20] This brings up a question of capital importance: what kind of obedience did the Old Covenant require in order for God to maintain his promise: perfect obedience to moral law or a consistent observance of it? The answer to this question is largely determined by the relationship that we see between the Covenant of Works and the Old Covenant. The Covenant of Works demanded perfect obedience to moral law; the transgressing of only one commandment was the transgression of the covenant and brought eternal damnation. Was this the case for the Old

God also promises to be the God of his people and that the latter will be "[…] a chosen people, a royal priesthood, a holy nation" (1 Pet. 2.9), but, contrarily to the Old Covenant, under the New Covenant this promise is unconditional: "I will be their God, and they will be my people. […] "For I will forgive their wickedness and will remember their sins no more." (Jer. 31.33-34). To be God's people, under the New Covenant, is guaranteed by the forgiveness of sins obtained by the mediator of this covenant; this is why Christ is presented as the one who is its guarantor (Heb. 7.22). To be the people of God, under the Old Covenant, was conditional on the obedience of this people. What is more, to have the Lord as one's God under the Old Covenant did not confer the same blessings as under the New Covenant: the first guaranteed earthly blessings, the second, heavenly blessings: eternal life.

The third piece of evidence given by Ball comes from a deduction that he makes from the first commandment of the Decalogue which is found in a different form in Deuteronomy 6.4-5: "Hear, O Israel: The Lord our God, the Lord is one. Love the Lord your God with all your heart and with all your soul and with all your strength." Ball indicates that this commandment was the equivalent of believing in God to have life; exactly as under the New Covenant. We agree with Ball that this commandment ultimately demands faith in God as under the New Covenant (Heb. 11.6). However, Ball is wrong in concluding that because this commandment demanded conversion to God, the Old Covenant unconditionally gave what it demanded. It is precisely on this point that the New Testament presents the Law as being weak and lacking since it could not operate in sinners what it required from them (Heb. 8.7; Rom. 8.3). It is also precisely on this point that the New Covenant is radically distinct from the Old since it gives what God orders. Thomas Patient writes: "Consider well, that in this covenant [the New Covenant] there is nothing that He requires, but He engages Himself to enable

Covenant? We will look at this question in detail in point 3.2 on the nature of the Old Covenant.

us to accomplish."[21] However, well before Thomas Patient, the apostle Paul wrote: "because through Christ Jesus the law of the Spirit who gives life has set me free from the law of sin and death. 3 For what the law was powerless to do because it was weakened by the flesh" (Rom. 8.2-3). The New Covenant successfully produces salvation in all its members, because it is unconditional.[22]

Faced with these difficulties, several paedobaptists were unable to consider the Mosaic Covenant as being unconditional. This was the case with Samuel Petto who writes:

> It is a conditional grant, it promises nothing but upon the condition of obedience. Exod. xix. Verse 5. *If ye will obey my voice, and keep my covenant, then ye shall be a peculiar treasure.*—All is upon an *if*. So, Levit. xxvi. 3,4,&c. *If ye walk in my statutes, and keep my commandments, and do them, then will I give you rain,* &c. The like in many other places; all promises run there upon the condition of keeping his commandments.[23]

Obviously, if the Sinaitic Covenant was conditional and if its promises depended on the obedience of its members, this presented a problem for the *one Covenant of Grace under two administrations* paradigm. How could one maintain that Israel was under a covenant of grace all the while considering that the Law of Moses was a covenant of works? The answer to this question was the second solution.

---

[21] Thomas Patient, *The Doctrine of Baptism, And the Distinction of the Covenants,* chapter 7 (around two-thirds of the way through the chapter).

[22] A fourth piece of evidence deserves to be examined. Ball affirms that it is evident that the Old Covenant was a covenant of grace since it was a covenant of redemption wherein one saw the doctrine of substitution in sacrifices as well as in the expiation and the forgiveness of sins. This point will be the main focus when we examine the nature of the Old Covenant in point 3.2, but for the moment, let us be content to remember that the Old Covenant, which did not offer the grace of salvation in itself, pointed typologically to this grace towards which it led. (Gal. 3.24).

[23] Samuel Petto, *The Great Mystery of the Covenant of Grace,* Stoke-on-Trent, Tentmaker Publications, 2007 (1820), p. 94.

1.2.2. Solution 2: the Mosaic Covenant was distinct from the Covenant of Grace concluded with Abraham

In order to be able to maintain the paedobaptist model of the Covenant of Grace while recognizing that the Mosaic Covenant was a conditional covenant, certain paedobaptists radically separated the Abrahamic Covenant from the Sinaitic Covenant. They saw the first in the same way as the Presbyterians saw the Covenant of Grace (i.e. administered under two mixed covenants) and they saw the second in the same way as the Baptists saw the Old Covenant (i.e. one conditional covenant, temporary and typological that did not give eternal life). This solution was especially developed by Samuel Petto[24]; it corresponds in great part to the understanding of paedobaptist theologians of today[25] who recognize the conditionality of the Mosaic Covenant while maintaining the one Covenant of Grace under two administrations. Petto writes:

> [I]t never saith, that the Covenant made with Abraham *is abolished*, but the contrary; declaring that the Law coming 430 years after could not disanull it. Also in Gospel times, they are said to be Children of the Covenant. Act. 3.25. And hence all

---

[24] Michael Brown deals with Petto's thought on the Mosaic Covenant in an entire chapter, cf. *Christ and the Condition*, pp. 87-104.

[25] The collective work edited by Bryan D. Estelle, J. V. Fesko and David VanDrunen, *The Law Is Not Of Faith*, is a good example. In this work, the different paedobaptist authors try to establish that the doctrine of republication (that is the Mosaic Covenant contains a republication of the Covenant of Works) is in tune with the reformed tradition. Another example is Michael Horton who summarizes his understanding of the conditional and unconditional nature with regards to the covenants concluded with Adam, Abraham and Moses in the following way: "If it is wrong to say that the Sinai covenant is simply identical to the Abrahamic covenant of grace, it is not quite right to say that the Sinai covenant (hence, the theocracy generally) is nothing more than a republication of the original covenant of works made to Adam before the fall." *God of Promise, Introducing Covenant Theology,* Grand Rapids, Baker, 2006, p. 54. John Murray, for his part, affirms that it is between the Abrahamic and the New Covenant that there are identical qualities: "The New Covenant in respect of its being a covenant does not differ from the Abrahamic as a sovereign administration of grace." *The Covenant of Grace*, Phillipsburg, P&R, 1953, p. 27.

those notions, that the Covenant made with Abraham, was a covenant of works, a legal temporal one, or mixt his natural seed, having but temporal promises by it in the land of *Canaan*, or a typical Covenant, I say these, as not true, vanish and come to nothing. And it is very considerable that in that Covenant with *Abraham*, the Lord promiseth *to be a God to him and his Seed after him*, Gen. 17.7. and then a Second time, with that temporal promise of the Land of *Canaan* to his Seed, he twisteth this, v.8. *and I will be their God.* So that visibly he is a God to the same Seed, which he promiseth the Land of Canaan too; and for him to be a God to any, is far greater than any temporal good whatsoever[26].

By separating the Abrahamic and Sinaitic Covenants (at least implicitly), Petto recognized without difficulty that the New Testament presented an Old Covenant that did not justify but condemn, that was temporary and replaced by the New Covenant. To this effect, Petto's understanding was identical to that of the Baptists. However, Petto was a paedobaptist who largely supported the Presbyterian model of the Covenant of Grace such as it was examined in the last chapter. The great distinction between Petto's thinking consisted in completely isolating the Abrahamic Covenant as a covenant of grace. According to him, the covenant concluded with Abraham offered the grace of salvation (Gal. 3.18) and, evidently, included the natural posterity of its members. It was therefore, according to Petto, a mixed covenant, some receiving the internal substance of this covenant, others being only under its external administration. It goes without saying that this Covenant of Grace, concluded with Abraham and his posterity, was the same as the New Covenant; only the external administration changed.

It is important to mention that Petto did not consider the Old and New Covenants as two administrations of the same covenant, but as two distinct covenants. He writes: "That new or better covenant is distinct from that at mount Sinai. It is usually said, that they are two administrations or dispensations of the same covenant: I think, they

---

[26] Samuel Petto, *Infant Baptism of Christ's Appointment*, p. 31-32.

are not merely one and the same covenant, diversely administered, but they are two covenants."[27] However, he affirms that the Abrahamic Covenant was the Covenant of Grace; the same that we find in the New Testament. In response to Thomas Grantham who opposed this view, Petto writes:

> And whereas Mr. *Grantham denieth that the Covenant*, Gen. 17. *is a Gospel-Covenant, or a covenant of grace,*

> This *is his gross errour; for the Apostle proveth Justification in Gospel-Times to be by Grace from this Covenant with* Abraham, Rom 4. 1, 2, 3, 4, 16, 17.

> This is the very Ground which his Argument is built upon. viz. *That we under the Gospel are justified in the same way that Abraham was, and therefore by grace*: By the promise, and not by the Law. [...]

> Doth Mr. *Grantham* think that the Apostle would seek to prove our Justification by an abrogated Covenant, and a legal one too, as he would have this be?[28]

If the covenant of circumcision given to Abraham was unconditional and should be radically separated from the Sinaitic Covenant, How did Petto explain this affirmation of the apostle Paul: "Again I declare to every man who lets himself be circumcised that he is obligated to obey the whole law" (Gal. 5.3). Paul seemed to draw a strong connection between circumcision (Abrahamic Covenant) and the Law (Mosaic Covenant). Petto avoided the difficulty by affirming that Paul was following the logic of the Judaizers without endorsing this logic:

---

[27] Samuel Petto, *The Great Mystery of the Covenant of Grace*, p. 103. Notice, however, that Petto precisely designates the Mosaic covenant. What he says does not apply to the Abrahamic covenant.

[28] Samuel Petto, *Infant-Baptism Vindicated from the Exceptions of Mr. Thomas Grantham*, London, Printed by T.S. for Ed. Giles, 1691, p. 17.

For either it speaketh of it in the Sense of the False Prophets, who urge Circumcision—for Justification and Salvation; And thus if Men should urge any Duty, even Baptism, upon such a legal Ground, it would make them Debtors to the whole Law. *Or it imports, that neither Circumcision, nor any Works of the Law, do profit, unless all be performed*; for the Law promised nothing but upon perfect Obedience, Gal. 3.10. Rom. 10.5.[29]

In separating the Abrahamic Covenant from the Mosaic Covenant, the paedobaptists like Petto affirmed the continuity of the first and the abolition of the second under the New Covenant. Since the Abrahamic Covenant included children and the New Testament uses this covenant as a foundation for the Scriptures, would not the paedobaptist position be greatly reinforced? B.B. Warfield writes: "God established His church in the days of Abraham and put children into it. They must remain there until He puts them out. He has nowhere put them out. They are still then members of His Church and as such entitled to its ordinances."[30]

The Baptists did not only simply have to prove that the Presbyterian model of the Covenant of Grace was faulty, but even more specifically, they had to demonstrate that the Presbyterian understanding of the Abrahamic Covenant and of its relationship with the other covenants was also faulty. This is exactly what Nehemiah Coxe undertook in *A Discourse of the Covenants that God made with men before the Law*. In this treatise, Coxe attempts to demonstrate that the Presbyterians had an erroneous understanding of the Abrahamic Covenant. Let us compare their understandings.

---

[29] *Ibid.*, p. 18.

[30] B. B. Warfield, *Studies in Theology*, (vol. 9 of *The Works of B. B. Warfield*; 1932; repr., Grand Rapids: Baker, 1981), 9:408. Quoted by Richard L. Pratt, *Baptism as a Sacrament of the Covenant*, p. 71.

2. THE ABRAHAMIC COVENANT

A cursory reading of Chapter 3 of Paul's Epistle to the Galatians could leave the impression that Samuel Petto's understanding was correct since in it, Paul opposes the Abrahamic Covenant and the Mosaic Covenant attributing grace to the first and works and the Law to the second.

> [17]What I mean is this: The law, introduced 430 years later, does not set aside the covenant previously established by God and thus do away with the promise. [18] For if the inheritance depends on the law, then it no longer depends on the promise; but God in his grace gave it to Abraham through a promise. (Gal. 3.17-18)

Paul clearly affirms that it is through the Abrahamic Covenant that God promised his grace and that the Mosaic Covenant which came about 430 years later did not bring the inheritance nor did it replace the Abrahamic Covenant. The paedobaptists understood from this passage that the Abrahamic Covenant was the Covenant of Grace, the covenant through which God grants his grace to Abraham and his posterity, and that the Judaizers were mistaken in demanding obedience to the Law of Moses as a condition in order to obtain the inheritance.[31] The Presbyterian paradigm of the Covenant of Grace

---

[31] The paedobaptists went even further by saying that in this passage, the apostle Paul in no way describes the nature of the Old Covenant, but only the false conception that the Judaizers had of it. Herman Witsius declares: "The design of the apostle therefore, in that place, is not to teach us, that the covenant of mount Sinai was nothing but a covenant of works, altogether opposite to the gospel-covenant; but only that the gross Israelites misunderstood the mind of God, and basely abused his covenant; as all such do, who seek for righteousness by the law." *The Economy of the Covenants*, vol. 2, p. 185. It is true that the Judaizers were mistaken in trying to gain justification through the Law rather than by faith (Rom. 9.31-32), but they were not mistaken as to the nature of the Law. Nowhere does the apostle Paul contest their understanding of the Law; on the contrary, he approves of it (Gal. 5.1-4; Rom. 10.5). Paul faults them for making a wrongful usage of the Law and for rejecting faith in favour of works in order to obtain justification.. The mistake of the Judaizers consisted in their believing that a sinner could be justified by the Law and not that the Law could justify (it could justify a righteous person). Facing the condemnation of the Law, the Judaizers

was confirmed by this interpretation: the Covenant of Grace that God concluded with Abraham included his physical posterity; the Covenant of Grace was, therefore, a Covenant of a mixed nature in which one entered at birth.

The Baptists were partially in agreement with the Presbyterian interpretation of this passage. They recognized that Paul exposed the legalistic error of the Judaizers by basing his argument on the fact that the promised inheritance was only granted by the grace of God and that this grace was given to Abraham when God made a covenant with him; the Law which had come into existence 430 years before did not replace grace as a method to obtain the inheritance. However, the Baptists did not support the Presbyterian paradigm of the Covenant of Grace which wanted the latter to include the physical posterity of Abraham and of believers. Instead, they applied their own paradigm of the Covenant of Grace (revealed/concluded) to this passage: the Covenant of Grace was revealed to Abraham, but the formal covenant that God concluded with him was not the Covenant of Grace. What is more, the text (Gal. 3.17-18) does not affirm that God gave his grace to Abraham through the covenant, but through the promise. In other words, the Abrahamic Covenant contained a promise; this promise was the revelation of the Covenant of Grace. The Abrahamic Covenant did include the physical posterity of Abraham, but it was not in the Covenant of Grace even if it was in a covenant that revealed the grace of God by way of a promise.

The paedobaptists, by applying the distinction between the substance and the administration of the Covenant of Grace, conceived that all the members of the Abrahamic Covenant did not benefit from the grace of God even if they were all under the same Covenant of Grace. The Baptists, by applying the distinction between the revelation and the conclusion of the Covenant of Grace, conceived that all the members of the Abrahamic Covenant did not

---

should have found hope in God's mercy offered by faith in Jesus Christ, the righteous one. For a more complete answer cf. Jeffrey Johnson, *The Fatal Flaw of the Theology Behind Infant Baptism*, p. 90ff.

benefit from the grace of God, because the Covenant of Grace was not concluded with the members of this covenant. The Covenant of Grace was revealed and only those who, like Abraham, believed, participated in the Covenant of Grace manifested in the Abrahamic Covenant. Consequently, the Baptists had a fundamentally different understanding of the Abrahamic Covenant than that of the Presbyterians. Let us examine these distinctions.

2.1. The duality of the Abrahamic Covenant

The Scriptures mention several dual principles. Regarding the covenant concluded with Abraham, the Scriptures also present a dualism. Abraham possesses a physical posterity as well as a spiritual posterity (Rom. 9.6-8; Gal. 4.22-31); there is an external circumcision of the flesh and an internal circumcision of the heart (Rom. 2.28-29); there is a promised land here on earth and a heavenly kingdom (Heb. 11.8-10). The Baptist pastor Hercules Collins revealed this truth in his catechism: "We must know the Covenant made with Abraham had two parts: first, a spiritual, which consisted in God's promising to be a God to Abraham, and all his Spiritual-Seed in a peculiar manner [...] "[32]

The paedobaptists and the Baptists mutually recognized this dualism, but in a completely different way. The paedobaptists considered this dualism within one covenant. According to them, this covenant included a physical reality, external and earthly, combined with a spiritual reality, internal and celestial, exactly as in their understanding of the Covenant of Grace wherein there was an internal substance and an external administration. The paedobaptists made a distinction between these two realities, but they refused to separate them into two distinct covenants. John Ball applied this paradigm in order to unite the physical and spiritual aspects of the

---

[32] Collins pursues in also presenting the physical and natural aspect of the Abrahamic covenant. James Renihan (ed.) "An Orthodox Catechism: Being the Sum of Christian Religion, Contained in the Law and Gospel," *True Confessions: Baptist Documents in the Reformed Family*, Owensboro, Reformed Baptist Academic Press, 2004, p. 257.

Abrahamic Covenant: "And therein the inward force and vertue of the [Abrahamic] Covenant is to be distinguished from the outward administration."[33] Although they recognized that the posterity of Abraham was both physical and spiritual at the same time, the paedobaptists refused to see two posterities, because, according to them, Abraham had only one posterity made up of the mixed people of the Covenant of Grace. This point was crucial, because if Abraham had two distinct posterities, the Baptists were right to not mix the natural (unregenerate) posterity and the spiritual (regenerate) posterity of Abraham. Inversely, if Abraham had only one mixed posterity, the paedobaptists were right to include those who were saved and those who were not saved in the Covenant of Grace. Samuel Petto had understood this critical concern:

> Hence see the true meaning of Gal. 3.16. *To Abraham and his seed were the Promises made: he saith not unto seeds, as of many, but as of one, and to thy seed, which is Christ*: i.e. Always *Abraham* had but one seed, Christ, and those that are Christ's, and are of the Faith as to Justification, he never had two seeds for that end; in the times of the Old Testament there was but one seed, not two seeds, one by the Law, and another by Promise, but only one in Christ by Promise [...]
>
> And so it is not in the least mentioned to exclude Infants, as a fleshly seed, from an ecclesiastical seed, nor to repeal any priviledge or limit to cut them off from what they had before the coming of Christ [...] [34]

The paedobaptists refused to separate the dualities of the Abrahamic Covenant in order to preserve their model of the Covenant of Grace which integrated these dualities. The Covenant of Grace, to include children, had to include both earthly and heavenly realities at the same time. Baptist theologians understood that if they kept these dualities united in the same covenant, they no

---

[33] John Ball, *A Treatise of the Covenant of Grace*, p. 48.
[34] Samuel Petto, *Infant Baptism of Christ's Appointment*, p. 37-38.

longer had any reason to refuse the Presbyterian model of the Covenant of Grace. In fact, if the Covenant of Grace revealed to Abraham included both his physical and spiritual posterity at once, why would it have been otherwise under the New Covenant? Therefore, not only did Baptist theology make the distinction between the physical and spiritual posterities of Abraham, but it also strictly separated them into two separate categories. The Baptists saw two posterities in Abraham, two inheritances and consequently two covenants.

2.1.1. Two posterities and two covenants in Abraham

Galatians 4.22-31 constitutes a key passage of Baptist federalism. In it we read:

> [22]For it is written that Abraham had two sons, one by the slave woman and the other by the free woman. [23]His son by the slave woman was born according to the flesh, but his son by the free woman was born as the result of a divine promise. [24]These things are being taken figuratively: The women represent two covenants. One covenant is from Mount Sinai and bears children who are to be slaves: This is Hagar. [25]Now Hagar stands for Mount Sinai in Arabia and corresponds to the present city of Jerusalem, because she is in slavery with her children. [26]But the Jerusalem that is above is free, and she is our mother. [27]For it is written: "Be glad, barren woman, you who never bore a child; shout for joy and cry aloud, you who were never in labor; because more are the children of the desolate woman than of her who has a husband." [28]Now you, brothers and sisters, like Isaac, are children of promise. [29]At that time the son born according to the flesh persecuted the son born by the power of the Spirit. It is the same now. [30]But what does Scripture say? "Get rid of the slave woman and her son, for the slave woman's son will never share in the inheritance with the free woman's son." [31]Therefore, brothers and sisters, we are not children of the slave woman, but of the free woman.

From this passage, Nehemiah Coxe understood, not that the posterity of Abraham was of a mixed nature, but that Abraham had two distinct posterities and that it was necessary to determine the inheritance of each of these posterities on the basis of their respective promises. He writes:

> Abraham is to be considered in a double capacity: he is the father of all true believers and the father and root of the Israelite nation. God entered into covenant with him for both of these seeds and since they are formally distinguished from one another, their covenant interest must necessarily be different and fall under a distinct consideration. The blessings appropriate to either must be conveyed in a way agreeable to their peculiar and respective covenant interest. And these things may not be confounded without a manifest hazard to the most important articles in the Christian religion.[35]

We have here a fundamental difference with the paedobaptist understanding of the Abrahamic Covenant. The aforementioned placed the natural and spiritual posterities of Abraham in the same Covenant of Grace; the first inheriting only the physical blessings of the covenant and the second benefiting also from the spiritual privileges. Coxe affirmed that it was not so. This is why he declares that since the Scriptures formally distinguished between the two posterities, one could not mix both up under the same covenant without compromising important doctrines.

This understanding was vigorously affirmed amongst all Baptist theologians and characterized their federalism from its origin. Spilsbury writes: "There was in *Abraham* at that time a spirituall seed and a fleshly seed. Between which seeds God ever distinguished through all their Generations."[36] On the allegory in Galatians 4, Henry Lawrence comments: "Here you have a distinction as it were of two *Abrahams*, a begetting *Abraham*, and a believing *Abraham*, and also of two seeds, the children of the flesh,

---

[35] Nehemiah Coxe, *A Discourse of the Covenants*, p. 72-73.
[36] John Spilsbury, *A Treatise Concerning the Lawfull Subject of Baptisme*, p. 6.

that is by carnal generation onely, and the children of the promise."[37] A little further, Lawrence specified that only those who, like Isaac, were born of the promise, that is, believers, are in the Covenant of Grace and are considered children of God: "Now, saith he, those only, which according to that of which Isaac was a type, are born by promise, those & those only are counted for the seed, Rom. 9.8."[38] The Baptists considered that it was essential to separate Abraham's posterities in this way in order to understand certain key texts of the Scriptures: Rom. 9.6-8; 2.28-29; 11; Jn. 8.39; Mat. 3.9; Gal. 3.29; 4.22-31; 1 Th. 2.15-16.

If Abraham had two distinct posterities and non-mixed and if they were in a relationship with God by way of the covenant, these two posterities had to find themselves in two distinct covenants. Consequently, several Baptists considered that God had concluded two covenants in Abraham: the Covenant of Grace in Genesis 12 with Abraham and his spiritual posterity (the believers) and the covenant of circumcision in Genesis 17 with Abraham and his natural posterity (the circumcised).[39] This does not mean that the

---

[37] Henry Lawrence, *Of Baptism*, p. 90.

[38] *Ibid.*, p. 91.

[39] Jeffrey Johnson, in *The Fatal Flaw*, rejects the separation that Nehemiah Coxe and other Baptists made within the Abrahamic covenant: "Unlike Coxe, I hold that God's promises to Abraham in Genesis 12 and 17 cannot be separated. I believe that these promises recorded in these two chapters are a part of the same covenant. However, the Abrahamic covenant is in essence two covenants in one." (p. 216). On the next page, however, he specifies that he agrees with Coxe on the foundation: "Nevertheless, although I differ with Coxe upon this smaller point, I am in full agreement with his main premise; the Abrahamic covenant cannot be understood properly without differentiating and separating the two covenants, which spring forth from the promises given to him." Samuel Petto, for his part, had understood that he could not separate the two posterities of Abraham in two covenants without losing the mixed nature of the Covenant of Grace. This is why he writes: " *I mean that Covenant which Circumcision was a Token of,* Gen. 17. v.7 to 15. Indeed, this is the same Covenant, for substance, with that, Gen. 12. but in a new Edition", *Infant-Baptism Vindicated from the Exceptions of Mr. Thomas Grantham*, p. 6. At first glance, Petto and Johnson seem to be saying the same thing, that there are not two Abrahamic covenants, but only one. However, when it comes time to apply the dualism within the Abrahamic covenant, Petto is content to distinguish between the substance and the

Baptists saw two formal Abrahamic Covenants. The Baptists, as we
have seen, considered that the Covenant of Grace did not manifest
itself as a formal covenant before the establishing of the New
Covenant. They did not consider that the Covenant of Grace was
formally established with Abraham in Genesis 12, but that it was
only revealed and promised to him. They saw only one formal
Abrahamic Covenant: the Covenant of circumcision established in
Genesis 17, all the while clearly differentiating this covenant from
the promise (the Covenant of Grace) that God had previously made.
This distinction between the promise revealed to Abraham and the
Covenant concluded with Abraham is unequivocal for John
Spilsbury:

> Again, its called the promise, and not the Covenant; and we
> know that every promise is not a covenant: there being a large
> difference between a promise and a covenant. And now let it be
> well considered what is here meant by the promise, and that is
> Gods sending of the Messias, or the seed in whom the Nations
> should be blessed; and so the sending of a Saviour or Redeemer
> unto Israel.[40]

Thomas Patient also separated the promise (i.e. the Covenant of
Grace) from the covenant of circumcision: "This promise is quoted
by the apostle Paul as the Gospel Covenant in Rom. 4:3 in
opposition to the *Covenant of Circumcision entailed upon the flesh
or fleshly line of Abraham.*"[41] It is in this way that the Baptists
understood that there were two covenants with Abraham, not two
formal covenants, but a promise that revealed the Covenant of Grace
followed by the covenant of circumcision. In light of Galatians 4.22-

---

administration and maintains this dualism in the same Covenant of Grace, while
Johnson affirms that these two distinct realities (physical and spiritual) are
concretized by the two distinct and separate covenants: the Old and the New.
There is here a fundamental difference.
[40] John Spilsbury, *A Treatise Concerning the Lawfull Subject of Baptisme*, p. 26.
[41] Thomas Patient, *The Doctrine of Baptism, And the Distinction of the Covenants*,
beginning of chapter 8.

31, the theologians of the 1689 considered that the two covenants that came from Abraham (Hagar and Sara) were the Old and New Covenants. The covenant of circumcision, Hagar, corresponded to the Old Covenant; a covenant of works established with the physical posterity of Abraham. The covenant of the promise, Sara, corresponded to the New Covenant; the Covenant of Grace revealed to Abraham and concluded with Christ and the spiritual posterity of Abraham (Gal. 3.29).

The fundamental divergence between the Presbyterians and the Baptists regarding the Abrahamic Covenant was found here. The first did not view Ishmael and Isaac, Hagar and Sara, the promise and circumcision, the Old and the New Covenant separately. They united these dualities within the same Covenant of Grace that possessed at the same time a physical and spiritual reality, an internal substance and an external administration. This system was self sufficient, but it could not harmonize itself naturally with biblical data and, in particular, to the fact that there was not one, but two covenants in Abraham (Gal. 4.24).

The second, basing themselves on the exegesis of Galatians 4.22-31, separated the dualities contained in Abraham in such a way as to recognize that two covenants came from the patriarch. Here is how Nehemiah Coxe summarized the Baptist under-standing of this passage:

> After reading the context, you will observe that the allegory insisted on by the apostle is grounded on the historical verity that Abraham had a twofold seed.
>
> 1. One proceeded from him according to the ordinary course and by the strength of nature; the other was produced by virtue of a promise. The one was Ishmael by Hagar, a bond-woman; the other was Isaac by Sarah, a free-woman.
>
> 2. The bond-woman and her son had the precedence in time of conception and birth to the free-woman and her son.

3. In the process of time the son of the bond-woman who was born after the flesh persecutes the son of the free-woman who was born after the Spirit; that is, in the virtue of the promise. Because of this the bond-woman and her son are cast out of the family and Isaac remains there as the only heir of his father's blessing.

The apostle affirms that these things were ordered by God in a typical relationship to the gospel times and applies them as follows.

Hagar was a type of Mount Sinai and the legal covenant established there. Ishmael was a type of the carnal seed of Abraham under that covenant. Sarah was a type of the new Jerusalem, the gospel church founded on the covenant of grace. Isaac was a type of the true members of that church who are born of the Spirit, being converted by the power of the Holy Spirit for the fulfilling of the promise of the Father to Jesus Christ the mediator. And the ejection of Hagar and Ishmael was to prefigure the abrogation of the Sinaitic Covenant and the dissolving of the Jewish church-state so that the inheritance of spiritual blessings might be clearly passed down to the children of God by faith in Jesus Christ.[42]

Understanding the workings of the dualism of the Abrahamic Covenant is essential for every theological system. We believe that Presbyterian federalism and dispensationalism failed in this task by confusing the promises of the Covenant of Grace with the covenant of circumcision. The Presbyterians thereby made the Covenant of Grace mixed and the dispensationalists assigned a distinct and permanent status as people of God to the physical descendants of Abraham. In both cases, the spiritual and

---

[42] Nehemiah Coxe, *A Discourse of the Covenants*, p. 130-31.

permanent blessings were amalgamated with the earthly and temporary covenant of circumcision.[43]

It happens, however, that the Scriptures do not always distinguish between the physical-earthly and spiritual-heavenly aspect of the Abrahamic Covenant. Actually, these two realities with their respective blessings are often side by side in the Scriptures, to a point where one could believe that they are two realities of a same covenant, as in the Presbyterian understanding. The Baptists, conscious of this difficulty, explained that the two posterities of Abraham, along with their respective inheritances, although distinct, were intertwined throughout the Old Covenant. To this effect, Coxe writes:

> I have endeavored to distinctly discuss the promises given to Abraham, first those that belong to his spiritual seed and then those that pertain to his carnal seed. These promises, despite their different nature and importance, are frequently found intermixed in the same transaction of God with Abraham, as they are in the sacred history presented to us interwoven with one another.[44]

Let us examine this point.

2.1.2. *The intertwining of the two posterities under the Old Covenant*

Coxe admitted that certain promises made to the spiritual posterity of Abraham were sometimes presented in terms which led to the expectation of an immediate blessing for his natural posterity. Far from seeing this as evidence in favor of the mixed nature of the Covenant of Grace, Coxe saw it as a typology. He writes:

---

[43]Jeffrey Johnson also notices this error that the Presbyterians and Dispensationalists have in common: "Paedobaptists place their biological seed in a special relationship with God, while dispensationalists still place Abraham's biological seed in a special relationship with God." *The Fatal Flaw of the Theology Behind Infant Baptism*, p. 79, note 16.

[44] Nehemia Coxe, *A Discourse of the Covenants*, p. 122.

It will readily be granted that some of those promises that ultimately respect the spiritual seed and spiritual blessings are sometimes given to Abraham under the cover of those terms that have an immediate respect to his natural seed and temporal blessings as types of the other. [...] But only this much will fairly follow from it: that the apostle argues form the carnal seed as typical to the spiritual seed as typified by it.[45]

For example, Coxe saw this intertwining in the Exodus of Israel.[46] The deliverance from Egypt was an earthly redemption given to the physical children of Abraham. However, the Scriptures also present this event as a type of spiritual liberation of the Church. But this is not the same covenant, nor the same blessing, nor the same posterity. While the Covenant of Grace and the covenant of circumcision, earthly redemption and heavenly redemption, as well as the physical and spiritual posterities are intertwined in this event, it is absolutely necessary to separate them; otherwise, their respective natures will be altered.[47] Coxe explains:

At present it will suffice to remind you that there is no way of avoiding confusion and entanglements in our conception of these things except by keeping before our eyes the distinction between Abraham's seed as either spiritual or carnal, and of the respective promises belonging to each. For this whole covenant of circumcision given to the carnal seed, can no more convey spiritual and eternal blessings to them as such, that it can now enright [give a right to] a believer (though a child of Abraham) in their temporal typical blessings in the land of Canaan. Neither can I see any reason for assigning a covenant interest in all

---

[45] *Ibid.*, p. 76.

[46] *Ibid.*, p. 123.

[47] Thomas Patient notes that it is possible to be under a typological redemption while remaining under the wrath of God; like many Israelites who were delivered by God from Egypt without benefiting from the redemption of Jesus Christ (cf. *The Doctrine of Baptism, And the Distinction of the Covenants*, end of chapter 15). This remark is very pertinent in order to avoid confusing the blessings granted to the respective successions of Abraham.

typified spiritual blessings (as well as in the temporal blessings that were the types of them) to the carnal seed, and yet not admit the same covenant to convey temporal blessings to the spiritual seed. I say this since some conceive both are directly included in the same covenant and the promise of both was sealed with the same seal.

But the truth is, despite the relationship this covenant has to the covenant of grace, it yet remains distinct from it.[48]

The posterities of Abraham were, therefore, often intertwined in their manifestation, but they were always ontologically distinct. Another reason for this intertwining comes from the fact that the posterities of Abraham were not necessarily distinct when it came to their subjects. One and the same person could be both a part of the physical and spiritual descendancy of Abraham. This explains that two categories of promises could be made to the same people without these promises being the essence of the same Covenant of Grace. John Owen explains that this reality caused an overlapping of Abraham's posterities without their being confused because of it:

Answerably unto this twofold end of the separation of Abraham, there was a double seed allotted unto him; —*a seed according to the flesh*, separated to the bringing forth of the Messiah according unto the flesh; and *a seed according to the promise*, that is, such as by faith should have interest in the promise, or all the elect of God. Not that these two seeds were always *subjectively* diverse, so that the seed separated to the bringing forth of the Messiah in the flesh should neither in whole nor in part be also the seed according to the promise; or, on the contrary, that the seed according to the promise should none of it be his seed after the flesh. [...] But sometimes the same seed came under diverse considerations, being the seed of Abraham both according to the flesh and according to the promise; and sometimes the seed itself was diverse, those according to the flesh being not of the

---

[48] Nehemia Coxe, *A Discourse of the Covenants*, p. 93.

promise, and so on the contrary. Thus Isaac and Jacob were the seed of Abraham according unto the flesh, separated unto the bringing forth of the Messiah after the flesh, because they were his carnal posterity; and they were also of the seed of the promise, because, by their own personal faith, they were interested in the covenant of Abraham their father.[49]

Already in 1643, John Spilsbury had the same understanding. He declares that if the posterities of Abraham were distinct; the covenants issuing from him had to be equally so. He recognized, however, that certain blessings and promises were common to the two posterities:

> And as there was a distinction thus made by God in *Abrahams* seed before they were circumcised [...] Even so there must be the same respect observed also in the Covenant, and that because the Covenant comprehends divers things; and Circumcision was a seale unto them all. Some of which were proper unto both the seeds, and some not.[50]

That the physical and spiritual descendents of Abraham had received common promises did not mean that these promises had the same value for each of these posterities. For example, the promise of being their God, as we have seen above, had a different meaning depending on the covenant in which it was situated and also based on the posterity to whom it was made, as Edward Hutchinson writes: "Now to both seeds, doth God promise to be a God, but in a different manner and respect."[51]

Another important reason, we believe, that the Covenant of Grace was intertwined with the covenant of circumcision comes from God's placing his promise under the custody of the Old Covenant in order to preserve it (Gal. 3:23). From this moment, the promise (the Covenant of Grace) could no longer be separated from

---

[49] John Owen, *An Exposition of the Epistle to the Hebrews*, vol. 1, Carlisle, The Banner of Truth Trust, 1991, p. 121-22.
[50] John Spilsbury, *A Treatise Concerning the Lawfull Subject of Baptisme*, p. 7.
[51] Edward Hutchinson, *A Treatise Concerning the Covenant and Baptism*, p. 26.

the covenant of circumcision (the Old Covenant). We will develop this point further as we examine the Mosaic Covenant.

3. THE MOSAIC COVENANT

The covenant concluded between God and Israel in the Sinai desert was a progression of the covenant of circumcision. The Sinaitic Covenant was specifically concluded with the physical posterity of Abraham for the accomplishment of the promises of the Abrahamic Covenant. The natural posterity of Abraham was to inherit the Promised Land and the Sinaitic Covenant was made to this end. One could ask oneself if Baptist federalism, contrary to the Presbyterian approach, rendered all covenants with the physical posterity of Abraham futile. To be sure, if the Old Covenant was not the Covenant of Grace, if it had earthly bearings and regarded only the physical posterity of Abraham, why was this covenant made and why did it occupy such a preponderant position to the point where the spiritual posterity of Abraham was, by comparison, an insignificant leftover (Rom. 9.27)? Why was this useless covenant made (Heb. 7.18) when the Covenant of Grace was operational independent of it? Owen raises the same question:

> Suppose, then, that this New Covenant of grace was extant and effectual under the old testament, so as the church was saved by virtue of it, and the mediation of Christ in that respect, how could it be that there should at the same time be another covenant between God and them, of a different nature from this, accompanied with other promises, and other effects?[52]

---

[52] John Owen, *An Exposition of Hebrews 8:6-13*, p. 180. John Calvin also asks a similar question in discussing the differences between the Old and New Testaments: "But it is said, Whence this diversity, save that God chose to make it? Would it not have been as easy for him from the first, as after the advent of Christ, to reveal eternal life in clear terms without any figures, to instruct his people by a few clear sacraments, to bestow his Holy Spirit, and diffuse his grace over the whole globe?" *Institution*, II, XI, 14.

The apostle Paul asks the same question: "Why, then, was the law given at all?" (Gal. 3.19). This brings us to explain the specific goal of the Old Covenant according to Baptist theology.

3.1. The goal of the Old Covenant

[19]Why, then, was the law given at all? It was added because of transgressions until the Seed to whom the promise referred had come. The law was given through angels and entrusted to a mediator. [20]A mediator, however, implies more than one party; but God is one. [21]Is the law, therefore, opposed to the promises of God? Absolutely not! For if a law had been given that could impart life, then righteousness would certainly have come by the law. [22]But Scripture has locked up everything under the control of sin, so that what was promised, being given through faith in Jesus Christ, might be given to those who believe. [23]Before the coming of this faith, we were held in custody under the law, locked up until the faith that was to come would be revealed. [24]So the law was our guardian until Christ came that we might be justified by faith. (Gal. 3.19-24)

The goal of the covenant with the physical posterity of Abraham (i.e. The Old Covenant or the Law) was not futile since it consisted in leading to Christ. This end was accomplished in at least three ways, according to the seventeenth-century Baptist authors' understanding: (1) by preserving both the messianic lineage and the Covenant of Grace; (2) by pointing typologically towards Christ; (3) by imprisoning everything under sin in order that the only means to obtain the promised inheritance was through faith in Christ.

(1) God promised Abraham that the accomplishment of his promise, by which all nations would be blessed, would fulfil itself by his posterity, that is, Christ (Gal. 3.16). Consequently, the Abrahamic lineage until the Messiah had to be preserved by a covenant with the natural posterity of Abraham (Rom. 9.4-5). In accordance with Romans 9.5, John Spilsbury declares that Israel's privilege was to bring the promised Messiah and not to be in the

Covenant of Grace. [53] The point of the genealogical succession of Abraham was not to establish a perpetual principle in order to include the natural posterity of all the members of a covenant, but only to lead to his ultimate posterity who was, according to this interpretation his only posterity. Fred Malone writes: "However, the genealogical element of the historical Old Testament covenants was necessary only to bring forth the final physical seed of Abraham to whom the promises were made, Jesus Christ."[54] Once the end was met, the way leading to it had to end. Alan Conner writes:

> The genealogical principle of the Abrahamic Covenant has been brought to its climactic fruition. There is no longer any reason to continue it as a covenant principle since "the Seed" has come into the world. Christ is the last physical seed in Abraham's covenant line to whom the promises were made. There is no other physical seed beyond Christ to whom these promises are directed.[55]

Since Abraham's physical posterity existed by virtue of the covenant of circumcision (the Old Covenant), when the goal of the covenant was accomplished (leading to Christ through the preservation of Abraham's physical posterity), the covenant made with Abraham's natural descendents came to an end. On what basis can one maintain a genealogical succession once the Old Covenant was over? John Owen writes:

> That this *separation* and privilege [namely, the setting apart of Israel and its preservation by means of a covenant] was to cease when the end of it was accomplished and the Messiah exhibited, the very nature of the thing declares; for to what

---

[53] John Spilsbury, *A Treatise Concerning the Lawfull Subject of Baptisme*, p. 20-21.
[54] Fred Malone, *Baptism of Disciples Alone*, p. 69-70.
[55] Alan Conner, *Covenant Children Today: Physical or Spiritual?*, Owensboro, Reformed Baptist Academic Press, 2007, p. 18.

purpose should it be continued when that was fully effected
whereunto it was designed?[56]

Not only was the goal of the Old Covenant to ensure the
maintaining of the Abrahamic lineage until Christ, but the promise
(i.e. the Covenant of Grace) had to also be preserved within this
same covenant.[57] Thus, the Scriptures affirm: "What advantage,
then, is there in being a Jew, or what value is there in circumcision?
Much in every way! First of all, the Jews have been entrusted with
the very words of God." (Rom. 3.1-2). According to the apostle, the
covenant of circumcision was given specifically for the preservation
of the divine oracles (*logia*). These oracles included the revelation of
the Covenant of Grace. The Covenant of Grace was revealed and
promised to Abraham as well as to his descendents during the whole
duration of the Old Covenant, but it was not concluded before the
establishment of the New Covenant in Jesus Christ.

(2) The Old Covenant led to Christ by pointing typologically
towards Him. The paedobaptists just like the Baptists were
conscious that the earthly blessings offered by the Old Covenant
(the deliverance from Egypt, Canaan and the tabernacles, etc.) were
all types of spiritual blessings of the New Covenant. Herman
Witsius writes: "But we are to observe, that these external promises
were types of spiritual and heavenly things."[58] However, the
Presbyterians and the Baptists did not see this typology in the same
way: for the former, the type and reality were contained in the same
covenant, while for the latter, the type and reality constituted two
separate covenants. This brings us back to the two paradigms

---

[56] John Owen, *An Exposition of the Epistle to the Hebrews*, vol. 1, p. 122.
[57] On the basis of the writings of Jerôme and Ambroise, Henry Lawrence, *Of
Baptism*, p. 75f. affirms that circumcision was a distinctive mark of Israel to avoid
its being assimilated by other nations and thereby losing the promise before it
could be accomplished. Thomas Patient shares this same conception regarding the
goal of circumcision: "So that this Covenant of Circumcision was of *sealing use
to Abraham* to *confirm* this other covenant [Covenant of Grace] and a School
Master to *lead* to Christ," *The Doctrine of Baptism, And the Distinction of the
Covenants*, Chapter 9, second argument.
[58] Herman Witsius, *The Economy of the Covenants*, vol. 2, p. 151.

regarding the Covenant of Grace and their relationship with the Old and the New Covenants. The Old Covenant pointed toward Christ and to the realization of the promises under the New Covenant.

(3) The third way in which the Old Covenant led to Christ was by its condemning of sin. This point is particularly brought to the fore by the apostle in Galatians 3:

> [19]Why, then, was the law given at all? It was added because of transgressions until the Seed to whom the promise referred had come. The law was given through angels and entrusted to a mediator. [20] A mediator, however, implies more than one party; but God is one. [21] Is the law, therefore, opposed to the promises of God? Absolutely not! For if a law had been given that could impart life, then righteousness would certainly have come by the law. [22] But Scripture has locked up everything under the control of sin, so that what was promised, being given through faith in Jesus Christ, might be given to those who believe.

A parallel passage in Paul's epistles explains that the ministry of the Old Covenant was that of condemnation and death:

> [6]He has made us competent as ministers of a New Covenant— not of the letter but of the Spirit; for the letter kills, but the Spirit gives life. [7]Now if the ministry that brought death, which was engraved in letters on stone, came with glory, so that the Israelites could not look steadily at the face of Moses because of its glory, transitory though it was, [8]will not the ministry of the Spirit be even more glorious? [9]If the ministry that brought condemnation was glorious, how much more glorious is the ministry that brings righteousness! (2 Cor. 3.6-9)

Presbyterian federalism was a bit perplexed by such affirmations. To be sure, Presbyterianism saw the Old Covenant as a covenant of grace. This conception was difficult to conciliate with the idea that the goal of the Covenant of the Law was to shed light on sin and condemn it. Inversely, the Presbyterians could have objected that if the Old Covenant was really conditional, it would have been incompatible with God's promises to Abraham and the free giving of His grace. Is this not to this objection that Paul wishes to respond when writing: "Is the law, therefore, opposed to the promises of God" (Gal. 3.21)? According the apostle, the Law had to lead to Christ in leaving the sinner with no other refuge but the grace of God through faith. John Owen explains that the promise and the Law, while radically different from one another, were not opposed one against the other but converged towards Christ.

> "That although the law does thus rebuke sin, convince of sin, and condemn for sin, so setting bounds to transgressions and transgressors, yet did God never intend it as a means to give life and righteousness, nor was it able so to do." The end of the promise was to give righteousness, justification, and salvation, all by Christ, to whom and concerning whom it was made. But this was not the end for which the law was revived in the covenant of Sinai. For although in itself it requires a perfect righteousness, and gives a promise of life for that reason, ("He that does these things, he will live in them,") yet it could give neither righteousness nor life to any in the state of sin. See Rom. 8:3; 10:4. To that end the promise and the law, having diverse ends, they are not contrary to one another.[59]

This third way of leading to Christ corresponded to the understanding the Baptists had of the nature of the Old Covenant. They saw it as a covenant of works, that is, a covenant whose blessings or curses were determined by the obedience or the disobedience of its members. To close this chapter, let us examine the nature of the Old Covenant in more detail.

3.2. The Nature of the Old Covenant

In point 1.2.1 of this chapter, we saw that many Presbyterians viewed the Mosaic Covenant as being unconditional. However, certain paedobaptists, as well as all the Baptists, did not share this

---

[59] John Owen, *An Exposition of Hebrews 8:6-13*, p. 193.

point of view since they saw the Old Covenant as a covenant of works, i.e. a conditional covenant. In this section, we will examine the relationship between the Old Covenant and the Covenant of Works given to Adam.

The Covenant of Works concluded at Creation required man's perfect obedience. The blessing of this covenant depended entirely on the works of Adam, because it provided no mercy or expiation in case of disobedience, but only death. This was not the case with the Old Covenant. The Scriptures present this covenant as being a covenant of redemption; the Old Covenant was based on a priesthood (Heb. 7.11). In a certain way, it was planned that the people would sin and that it would subsist nonetheless thanks to the Levitical system of sacrifices. John Ball relies on the fact that the Old Covenant planned for the forgiveness of sins, something the Covenant of Works could never have done, to prove that it was not a covenant of works, but of grace.[60] Herman Witsius came to the same conclusion:

> The covenant made with Israel at mount Sinai was not formally the covenant of works, 1st. Because that cannot be renewed with the sinner, in such a sense as to say, if, for the future, thou shalt perfectly perform every instance of obedience, thou shalt be justified by that, according to the covenant of works. For, by this, the pardon of former sins would be presupposed, which the covenant of works excludes.[61]

Samuel Petto, who did consider the Mosaic Covenant as being conditional, recognized that it could not be strictly the same Covenant of Works established at Creation:

> [T]he covenant of works with the first Adam being violated, it was at an end as to the promising part; it promised nothing; after once it was broken, it remained in force only as to its threatening part, it menaced death to all the sinful seed of Adam, but admitted no other into it who were without sin, either to

---

[60] John Ball, *A Treatise of the Covenant of Grace*, p. 108.
[61] Herman Witsius, *The Economy of the Covenants*, vol. 2, p. 184.

perform the righteousness of it, or to answer the penalty; it had nothing to do with an innocent person, after broken, for it was never renewed with man again, as before.[62]

Nothing, under the Covenant of Works, provided for the reparation of sin through the substitution of a righteous person. In this way, the Old Covenant was very different from the Covenant of Works. Nevertheless, under the Old Covenant there was a principle belonging to the covenant made with Adam: "Keep my decrees and laws, for the person who obeys them will live by them" (Lev. 18.5).

How did the Baptists, and certain paedobaptists along with them, conceive the nature of the Old Covenant if it was not *the Covenant of Works* while being *a covenant of works*? What was the relationship between the Covenant of Works given to Adam and the Old Covenant made with Israel? Benjamin Keach affirms that there was, between the two of them, continuity but not uniformity:

> True, there was another Edition or Administration of it [the Covenant of Works] given to *Israel*. which tho' it was a covenant of works, *i.e. Do this and live*, yet it was not given by the Lord to the same End and Design, as the Covenant was given to our

---

[62] Samuel Petto, *The Great Mystery of the Covenant of Grace*, p. 131-32. John Owen explains that no matter the link that one establishes between the Covenant of Works and the Old Covenant, the latter was never given as a covenant of life (Gal. 3.21), as the Covenant of Works was for Adam: "The church of Israel was never absolutely under the power of that covenant as a covenant of life [Ga 3.21]; for from the days of Abraham, the promise was given to them and their seed. And the apostle proves that no law could afterwards be given, or covenant made, that should disannul that promise, Gal. 3:17. But had they been brought under the Old Covenant of works, it would have disannulled the promise; for that covenant and the promise are diametrically opposite. And moreover, if they were under that covenant, they were all under the curse, and so perished eternally: which is openly false; for it is testified of them that they pleased God by faith, and so were saved." *An Exposition of Hebrews 8:6-13*, p. 171. Most of those who thought of the Old Covenant as a covenant of works did not think that God had given this covenant so that Israel would try to obtain life by obeying the Law. The Old Covenant reaffirmed the Covenant of Works, but did so with a totally different goal in mind than when it was given to Adam (cf. note 31).

first parents, viz. It was not given to justifie them, or to give them eternal Life[63].

A few years later, Keach published a collection of sermons on the Covenant of Grace in which he reiterated that the Covenant of Works was reaffirmed by the Old Covenant, but to a different end than at the time of its initial proclamation:

> Though evident it is that God afterwards more clearly and formally repeated this Law of Works to the People of Israel [...] though not given in that Ministration of it for Life, as before it was to Adam; yet as so given, it is by St. Paul frequently called the Old Covenant, and the Covenant of Works, which required perfect Obedience of all that were under it[64].

This specification constituted an essential characteristic of Baptist federalism, specifically that the Covenant of Works, after the fall, was never again used, for the descendents of Adam, as "a law [...] that could impart life" (Gal. 3.21). This does not mean that the Covenant of Works had no further use, nor that it was absent from the covenants that God established with his people. On the contrary, it was reaffirmed, but in a new way; it was placed at the core of a covenant of redemption and was employed to different ends. According to this conception then, the Old Covenant was not exactly the equivalent of the Covenant of Works although it reaffirmed it. In agreement with the Covenant of Works, the Old Covenant demanded a perfect obedience to the Law of God,[65] but contrary to

---

[63] Benjamin Keach, *The Everlasting Covenant*, p. 7.

[64] Benjamin Keach, *The Display of Glorious Grace*, p. 15.

[65] The slightest disobedience to the Law constituted a sin punishable by death (Rom. 6.23), but not necessarily a transgression of the Old Covenant. It is necessary to make the distinction between the requirements of the Law of works affirmed under the Old Covenant and the requirements of the Old Covenant itself towards Israel. The maintaining of the Old Covenant depended on the Levitical priesthood (Heb. 7.11) and not on absolute obedience. God planned for his commandments to be transgressed while maintaining his covenant. J.R. Williamson writes: "If the obedience required had been absolute and perfect in heart, in speech and action, then the covenant would not have lasted until the end

the Covenant of Works, the Old Covenant was based on a sacrificial system for the redemption of sinners.[66] The Covenant of Works reaffirmed in the Old Covenant made this sacrificial system absolutely necessary since all sinners transgressed the law. However, the sacrifices of the Old Covenant could not accomplish the righteousness of the law effectively; that is why they only had a typological and temporary value. As long as they were offered, these sacrifices recalled that the requirements of the law were not satisfied, since sin still subsisted, and that this law weighed on the members of the Old Covenant like a curse (cf. Heb. 10.1-14). It is under this law that Christ was born (Gal. 4.4) and it is this same law

---

of the day it was declared. Instead, the obedience required was general and national in character. God graciously overlooked the many offenses. However, the covenant would be broken if Israel habitually sinned and were marked nationally as a rebellious people who disregarded God's Word." *From the Garden of Eden to the Glory of Heaven*, Amityville, Calvary Press, 2008, p. 115. (The same affirmation if made by Herman Witsius, *The Economy of the Covenants*, vol. 2, p. 184.). The Old Covenant was, therefore, not given to Israel as a covenant of life (Gal 3.21). However, it held this function for Christ. This is why Samuel Petto considered that the Old Covenant did not have the same function for Israel as for Christ. For Israel it was a national covenant by whose conditions Israel received blessings and curses in its land (Deut. 28). For Christ, it was a covenant of works for which He had to accomplish righteousness actively and passively (Rom. 5.18-20; 8.3-4; Gal. 3.13; 4.4-5). Petto writes: "The Sinai law was not given as a covenant of works to Israel. It was designed to be a covenant of works as to be accomplished by Jesus Christ, as will appear afterwards; but the end of the Lord was not that it should be so to Israel." *The Great Mystery of the Covenant of Grace*, p. 113. This point is crucial in understanding the nature of the Old Covenant, its relationship to the Covenant of Works, its requirements for Israel as the covenant people and its accomplishment in Jesus Christ as the last Adam. We do not have the space necessary to elaborate further on this point; we, therefore, refer our readers to Petto's work in Chapter VII titled *Of the Nature of the Mount Sinai Covenant*.

[66]After the fall, the Covenant of Works is no longer found as a law of life, because it would have been impossible for sinners to subsist within it and obtain life through it because of sin (cf. Rom. 8.3; Gal. 3.21). The Covenant of Works was maintained after the fall, thanks to the Old Covenant where it functioned on a new basis: a sacrificial system. This sacrificial system did not start with Aaron, but immediately after the fall and was in effect at the time of the patriarchs (Gn. 3.21; 4.4; 8.20; 22.13; 46.1), until it was fully developed in the Law of Moses.

(i.e. the Covenant of Works reaffirmed in the Old Covenant) that Christ fulfilled by his obedience (Rom. 5.19-20) and it is the curse of this law which he endured by his death (Gal. 3.13). Christ therefore accomplished the Old Covenant perfectly. John Owen summarizes the link between the Old Covenant, the Covenant of Works and its accomplishment in Christ:

> This covenant thus made [the Old Covenant], with these ends and promises, did never save nor condemn any man eternally. All that lived under the administration of it did attain eternal life, or perished forever, but not by virtue of this covenant as formally such. It did, indeed, revive the commanding power and sanction of the first covenant of works; and in that respect, as the apostle speaks, was "the ministry of condemnation," 2 Cor. 3: 9; for "by the deeds of the law can no flesh be justified." And on the other hand, it directed also to the promise, which was the instrument of life and salvation to all that did believe. But as to what it had of its own, it was confined to things temporal. Believers were saved under it, but not by virtue of it. Sinners perished eternally under it, but by the curse of the original law of works.[67]

Therefore, the Old Covenant was, for the people of Israel, a figurative covenant, earthly and conditional, that had to lead them to Christ and not to the Covenant of Works as such. The Old Covenant, while being different from the Covenant of Works, reaffirmed it, not so that Israel would look for life by this means, but so that Christ would accomplish it. The Old Covenant was, therefore, not only necessary to lead to Christ but it was necessary so that the later could accomplish salvation for God's Israel.[68] Samuel Petto explains this important point:

---

[67] John Owen, *An Exposition of Hebrews 8:6-13*, p. 197-98.

[68] This assertion is based on the notion that the Old Covenant did not have the same goal for Israel and for Christ. God did not place Israel under the Old Covenant as a law of life (Gal. 3.17-21); however, the principle of a law of life was contained in the Old Covenant (Lev. 18.5; Gal. 3.12). Nonetheless, only Christ could accomplish this law of life thereby changing the law of death to a law

Indeed, I think, one great end of God in bringing Israel under this Sinai covenant, was to make way for Christ, his being born or made under the law, in order to the fulfilling of it for us. I do not see how (by any visible dispensation) Jesus Christ could have been born actually under the law, if this Sinai covenant had not been made; for the covenant of works with the first Adam being violated, it was at an end as to the promising part; it promised nothing; after once it was broken, it remained in force only as to its threatening part, it menaced death to all the sinful seed of Adam, but admitted no other into it who were without sin, either to perform the righteousness of it, or to answer the penalty; it had nothing to do with an innocent person, after broken, for it was never renewed with man again, as before: therefore, an admitting an innocent person (as Jesus Christ was) into it, must be by some kind of repetition or renewing of it, though with other intendments than at first, viz. that the guilty persons should not fulfil it for themselves, but that another, a surety, should fulfil it for them.[69]

This explanation from Petto demonstrates how he himself and the Baptists considered that the Covenant of Works was reaffirmed with a different goal than at its first promulgation.[70] The Covenant of Works did not provide a substitution to satisfy its righteousness; no one could obey in Adam's place nor suffer his punishment. God, therefore, reaffirmed the Covenant of Works in another covenant that allowed for a righteous person to substitute himself for sinners.

---

of life through his death and his life (Rom. 8.2-4). The blessings and curses that Israel received from the Old Covenant were temporal while those that Christ received were eternal. The Old Covenant was typological for Israel, but absolutely real for Christ. However, these two different functions were not independent from one another since the Old Covenant had to lead Israel to Christ. It is true that God did not give the Old Covenant to Israel in view of justification through works (Rom. 9.31-32), but the law of works of this covenant demanded a perfect obedience nonetheless. Faced with this impossibility, all that was left to do was wait for the promised Messiah; this is what all the believers of this covenant did. For the others, it was a curse (Gal. 3.13).

[69] Samuel Petto, *The Great Mystery of the Covenant of Grace*, p. 131-32.
[70] See the last two Benjamin Keach quotes (notes 63 and 64).

Not only was the Old Covenant not *against* the promises of God (Gal. 3.21), but it was given specifically *for* the accomplishment of these promises (Gal. 3.22-24). Without being itself a covenant of grace, the Old Covenant was given because of the Covenant of Grace and with a view to its accomplishment. Is this what the apostle John wanted to underline by declaring: "Out of his fullness we have all received grace in place of grace already given. For the law was given through Moses; grace and truth came through Jesus Christ." (Jn. 1.16-17)? The Law given by Moses was a grace to lead to the grace accomplished by Jesus Christ.

CONCLUSION AND SUMMARY

Let us briefly summarize this chapter. The Baptists and the paedobaptists mutually recognized the cumulative aspect of the Old Covenant, specifically that it started informally after the fall until it became a formal covenant between God and the descendents of Abraham as a nation. However, Presbyterian federalism had great difficulty to reconcile its view of the whole Old Testament as an administration of the Covenant of Grace while the Mosaic Covenant had a strong legal propensity, punitive and conditional. Two solutions were elaborated by the Presbyterians of the time. The first: to present the Mosaic Covenant as an unconditional covenant by explaining its conditions as being the effect and not the condition of the promises. The second: to recognize the conditionality of the Mosaic Covenant by isolating it from the Abrahamic Covenant of Grace (thereby preserving the notion of a covenant of grace of mixed nature that included the natural posterity of its members).

This second solution represented a greater difficulty for the Baptists since the Presbyterian explanation of the Abrahamic Covenant justified their paradigm of the Covenant of Grace (substance/administration). This solution was even more persuasive since it seemed, at first glance, to have the full support of Galatians 3.15-18. Thus, the Baptists defined the Abrahamic Covenant carefully, in particular based on Galatians 4.22-31, and, in light of this passage, they reinterpreted Galatians 3.15-18.

The understanding of the Abrahamic Covenant constituted a breaking point between Baptist and paedobaptist federalism. It is difficult to determine if their respective understandings of the Abrahamic Covenant determined their own paradigm of the Covenant of Grace or if it was the opposite. Either way, the opposition between their federalism manifested itself concretely and fundamentally around the Abrahamic Covenant. The aforementioned presents a dualism between the promises of an earthly nature and those of a heavenly nature. The paedobaptists mixed the two in one same covenant of grace of mixed nature, while the Baptists strictly separated these two types of promises. The Baptists justified this separation based on the fact that Abraham had two heterogeneous posterities and that each of them inherited a covenant with different promises. His natural posterity received an earthly inheritance and was kept under the Old Covenant. His spiritual posterity received a heavenly inheritance through the New Covenant which, until its accomplishment, was in the state of a promise (revealed/concluded). Both of Abraham's posterities were, however, intertwined until the accomplishment of the promise which was temporarily placed under the protection of the Law (Gal. 3.23).

What brought us specifically to the Mosaic Covenant which was first presented at the beginning of this chapter as a progression of the covenant of circumcision. We then successively examined the goal and the nature of the Old Covenant (as accomplished by the Mosaic Covenant) from the perspective that it was not a covenant of grace, but a conditional covenant of works (according to the Baptist conception and that of a few seventeenth-century paedobaptists). We saw that the Old Covenant's goal was to lead to Christ in three ways: (1) in preserving both the messianic lineage and the Covenant of Grace; (2) by pointing typologically toward Christ; (3) by imprisoning everything under sin so that the only means to obtain the promised inheritance was through faith in Christ. This third point raised the question of the nature of the Old Covenant as a conditional covenant. We previously presented the understanding that Baptists had of the relationship between the creational Covenant of Works and the Sinaitic Covenant of the Law. The Baptist understanding of the nature of this covenant was founded on a distinction between the initial function of the Covenant of Works and its new function under the Old Covenant; this covenant had a function that was distinct, but inseparable, for Israel and for Christ.[71] This new function of the Covenant of Works under the Old Covenant gave Christ a covenantal frame to bring about redemption.

All that is left is for us to examine is the New Covenant in order to finish our presentation of seventeenth-century reformed, paedobaptist and credobaptist federalism.

---

[71] We must, however, emphasize that this last distinction was put forward mainly by Samuel Petto, a paedobaptist. Regarding the nature of the Old Covenant, its relationship to the Covenant of Words and its function for Israel and for Christ, see notes 31, 62, 65 and 68.

Chapter 4
The New Covenant

Our chapter on the New Covenant will be remarkably briefer than the two that preceded it since most of the differences between the Presbyterian and Baptist conceptions of the New Covenant have already been broached in Chapter 2 and implied in Chapter 3. In fact, the identity of the New Covenant cannot be separated from the Covenant of Grace which was largely examined in these two chapters. We will, therefore, not go back over the questions that were already covered in the theological comparisons of Chapter 2 which end up being comparisons between the two conceptions of the New Covenant. This chapter will mainly deal with the notion of the newness of the New Covenant. Was it indeed new? If so, in what way?

1. THE NEWNESS OF THE NEW COVENANT

It was dangerous to affirm that a covenant called new was not new. Such a statement was counter-intuitive and required a laborious demonstration. Yet, no Presbyterians believed that the New Covenant was new. Actually, their model of the Covenant of Grace led them to see an identity of substance between the Old and the New Covenants, the latter could not very well be new while having the same substance as the first. How did the paedobaptists explain that the Scriptures frequently present it as being a covenant that was new (Jer. 31.31-32; Lk. 22.20; 2 Cor. 3.6; Heb. 12.24)? They managed it by using the separation between the substance and the administration of the Covenant of Grace. Thus, the paedobpatists considered that the New Covenant was, in fact, simply a new administration and not a substantially different covenant. William Ames writes:

4. The testament is new in relation to what existed from the time of Moses and in relation to the promise made to the fathers. But it is new not in essence but in form. [...] Since the complete difference between the New Covenant and the old appeared only in the administration which came after Christ, this administration is properly termed the covenant and testament which is new.

5. This differs also from the former administration in quality and quantity.

6. Its difference in quality is in clarity and freedom.[1]

The newness of the New Covenant, according to this theological approach, was confined to the external aspects of the covenant and did not touch on its internal substance. This is exactly what the great reformed theologian Francis Turretin said: "It is called "new" not as to the substance of the covenant (which is the same in both) but: (1) as to the circumstances and mode [...] (2) as to the excellence and glory of this dispensation [...] (3) as to perpetual duration." [2] A little further on, Turretin takes into account the text in Jeremiah 31 that opposes the Old and New Covenants; he explains: "Although the Sinaitic and the legal covenants are opposed in Jer. 31 to the New Covenant, it is not necessary that this opposition should be as to essence, but it can be as to accidents or diversity of economy."[3]

The reading that Turretin did of this passage seems very uncertain. Michael Horton, a paedobaptist, rejects this interpretation:

---

[1] William Ames, *The Marrow of Theology*, p. 206.

[2] *Institutes of Elenctic Theology*, vol. 2, p. 232.

[3] *Ibid.*, p. 267. Several paedobaptists explained the adjective "new" (חֲדָשָׁה) of verse 31 with the idea of "renewal." Jeremiah would simply have been announcing the renewal of the Covenant of Grace already established under the Old Covenant. Most of the exegetes, including Calvin, are opposed to this interpretation. John Calvin, *Commentaries on the Epistle to the Hebrews*, p. 188; Alan Conner, *Covenant Children Today*, p. 36; Stephen J. Wellum, "Baptism and the Relationship Between the Covenants," *Believer's Baptism, Sign of the New Covenant in Christ*, Nashville, B&H Publishing Group, 2006, p. 141-42.

In fact, God firmly says through Jeremiah that this New Covenant "will not be like the covenant I made with their forefathers when I took them by the hand to lead them out of Egypt, *because they broke* my covenant, though I was a husband to them" (31:32 NIV). The point could not be clearer: the New Covenant is not a renewal of the Old Covenant made at Sinai, but an entirely different covenant with an entirely different basis.[4]

Not only does the text from Jeremiah 31 oppose the Old and New Covenants, but it also specifies the terms of that opposition: contrary to the Old, the New Covenant will not be violated.[5] The text, therefore, does not superficially oppose the external circumstances of the two covenants as Turretin would have wanted, but it opposes their very substance: one was "transgressable" because it was conditional while the other will be "intransgressable" because it will be unconditional. John Owen, in agreement with Baptist theology, explains that this unconditional nature constituted the newness of the New Covenant:

> A covenant properly is a compact or agreement on certain terms mutually stipulated by two or more parties. As promises are the foundation and rise of it, as it is between God and man, so it comprises also precepts, or laws of obedience, which are prescribed to man on his part to be observed. *But in the description of the covenant here annexed* [the New Covenant], *there is no mention of any condition on the part of man, of any terms of obedience prescribed to*

---

[4] Michael Horton, *God of Promise*, p. 53. Horton can affirm such a thing while being a paedobaptist since he separates the Abrahamic covenant from the Mosaic covenant. Thus, according to his theology, the New Covenant is radically different from the Mosaic covenant, but not from the Abrahamic covenant. We saw in the previous chapter how the Baptists responded to this dichotomy and why they rejected the Presbyterian understanding of the Abrahamic covenant.

[5] We suppose that Horton put this part of the verse in italics, in the last quote, precisely to underline in what way the New Covenant would be different from the Old.

him, but the whole consists in free, gratuitous promises, as we will see in the explication of it.[6]

The unconditional nature constitutes the radically new and unique element of the New Covenant. For the credobaptists, the New Covenant was radically new since no other formal covenant before it was unconditional.[7]

1.1. The Unconditional Nature of the New Covenant

The promises of the Old Covenant were preceded by an "if" that made them conditional on man's obedience, while the promises of the New Covenant were marked by a divine monergism:

> [33]"This is the covenant I will make with the people of Israel after that time," declares the Lord. "I will put my law in their minds and write it on their hearts. I will be their God, and they will be my people. [34] No longer will they teach their neighbour, or say to one another, 'Know the Lord,' because they will all know me, from the least of them to the greatest," declares the Lord. "For I will forgive their wickedness and will remember their sins no more." (Jer. 31.33-34)

The three elements that make up the substance of the New Covenant are works supremely operated by God and are presented in the indicative mood, not the conditional. None of these promises

---

[6] John Owen, *An Exposition of Hebrews 8:6-13*, p. 259. Italics added.

[7] One of the reasons that the paedobaptists had difficulty admitting the newness of the New Covenant came from the fact that its substance, salvation by grace in Jesus Christ, was given to believers from the fall. How could it be new (meaning different) rather than a renewal of the grace that was already granted so long ago? We have seen in Chapter 2 in what way the Baptists responded to this question by distinguishing between the revelation of the New Covenant (Covenant of Grace) as a promise and its formal establishment as a covenant. We have also seen that this notion is supported by the exegesis of Hebrews 9.15 (cf. Section 3.3 of Chapter 2).

depends on a condition that had first to be met by man. The unconditional nature of this covenant made it a radically New Covenant. Thomas Patient explains that what made the New Covenant "intransgressable," contrary to the Old Covenant which could be transgressed (Gen. 17.14), was this unconditional character:

> For, as I have shown before, it is impossible that the New *Covenant can be broken because it is an absolute covenant made on no condition to be fulfilled by the creature. But the Lord works "both to will and to do of His good pleasure" in this covenant.* Therefore, "*it is not in him that willeth, nor in him that runneth, but in God Who shows mercy.*"[8]

However, the Baptists did not conceive of the unconditional nature of the New Covenant as coming from the abolition of the Covenant of Works. On the contrary, the New Covenant was unconditional, according to them, since the Covenant of Works was accomplished. Thus, the New Covenant was unconditional for all its members, but it was not for its mediator: Christ. Benjamin Keach expresses this understanding:

> 1. As it refers to Christ, or to his part, and Work therein; and as thus it was a Conditional Covenant, Christ receives all for us, wholly upon the account of his own Desert, or Merits.

> 2. But whatsoever we receive by virtue of this Covenant, it is wholly in a way of Free Grace and Favor, through his Merits, or through that Redemption we have by his Blood: But take it either ways, 'tis of Grace.[9]

---

[8] Thomas Patient, *The Doctrine of Baptism, And the Distinction of the Covenants*, chapter 9, argument 6. The italics are from the author.

[9] Benjamin Keach, *The Display of Glorious Grace*, p. 173. Similarly, John Bunyan, in a section entitled "The conditions of the New Covenant" presents the conditional aspect of this covenant; in another section entitled "Christ completely fulfilled the conditions of the New Covenant," he demonstrates that it is not the believer, but only Christ who guarantees the success of this covenant and ensures

If the blessings of the New Covenant were guaranteed by Christ (Heb. 7.22), how could one conceive, as did the Presbyterians, that the New Covenant was just as "transgressable" as the Old? This could be explained in two ways: either the Presbyterians did not believe that Christ alone guaranteed the promises of the New Covenant, but that its members had something to do with their accomplishment; or they did not believe that Christ's mediation was absolutely effective in unconditionally guaranteeing the blessings of the New Covenant to its members, since they considered that one could fall from it. In the first case, one sacrificed the unconditional nature, in the second, one sacrificed the effectiveness. To avoid these two pitfalls, the paedobaptists had recourse to their division between the substance and the administration of the covenant. Let us examine their reasoning. Thomas Blake starts by trying to prove the "transgressability" of the New Covenant:

> This is farther clear in that Text of the Apostle, Heb. 10 29. *Of how much sorer punishment, suppose ye, shall he be thought worthy, who hath trodden under foot the Son of God, and hath counted the blood of the covenant, wherewith he was sanctified, an unholy thing, and hath done despite unto the Spirit of grace?* Where we see those that are sanctified with the blood of the Covenant do tread under foot the Son of God, and count his blood an unholy thing, have an esteem of it, as that which is common, and never devoted at all to God. These must needs be granted to be wicked, yet cannot be denied to be in Covenant, being sanctified with the blood of the Covenant.[10]

Blake's objective, based on Hebrews 10.29, was to demonstrate that the New Covenant, like the Old, was "transgressable" since a covenant of this nature was necessary for him in order to include the posterity of believers. We believe, however, that the foundation of this proof rests on a faulty interpretation of this verse, caused mainly

---

its blessings to its members. *The Doctrine of the Law and Grace Unfolded*, p. 524, 534.

[10] Thomas Blake, *Vindiciae Foederis,* p. 198.

by a bad translation of this same verse. Grammatically, this verse can be translated as Blake read it. Theologically however, this translation is impossible. How could someone who had been sanctified by the blood of Christ (the blood of the covenant) perish? Another translation is preferable, one that is grammatically and theologically true. This translation is the following: "How much more severely do you think someone deserves to be punished who has trampled the Son of God underfoot, who has treated as an unholy thing the blood of the covenant, by which it was sanctified, and who has insulted the Spirit of grace?" The subject of the verb sanctified, from a grammatical point of view, could either be "someone [...] who has trampled the Son of God underfoot" or "the covenant". The third person singular of the verb ἀγιάζω (to sanctify) does not indicated the gender; it could, therefore, be masculine of feminine. The question that any exegete must ask himself is: what was sanctified by the blood of Christ? The correct answer is: the New Covenant[11]! (Cf. Luke 22.20), a covenant that certain people, to their own perdition, trample underfoot as if it were profane.

Blake was, however, conscious that if this verse, according to the translation of the King James Version which he used, played in favour of his theology (by proving that there were "unconverted" people in the New Covenant as in the Old), it also posed a serious soteriological problem for him: was it possible to lose salvation? Presbyterian federalism, therefore, still found itself faced with the same dilemma between the unconditional nature and the effectiveness of the New Covenant. Blake was conscious of this difficulty that he resolved in the following way:

> How the reprobate can be said to be sanctified by the bloud [sic] of the Covenant ? answers; *There is a sanctification to the purifying of the flesh, and a sanctification to the purifying of the conscience from dead works, to serve the living God* Hebr. 9.13, 14. *The sanctification externall to the purifying of the flesh consisteth in the mans separation from the world,*

---

[11] Paul Ellingworth confirms the grammatical correctness of our exegesis: "Grammatically, the subject could be the covenant". *The Epistle to the Hebrews*, NIGTC, Grand Rapids, Eerdmans, 1993, p. 541

*and dedication unto Gods service, by calling and Covenant, common to all
the members of the visible Church, and it is forcible thus far, as to bring a
man into credit and estimation as a Saint before men, and unto the common
priviledges of the Church, whereupon, as men, so God also speaketh unto
him, and of him as one of his people, and dealeth with him in his external
dispensation as with one of his own people. In this sense all the
Congregation of Israel, and every one of them is called holy [...]*[12]

The paedobaptist solution rested entirely on the idea that the
members of the New Covenant, like those of the Old, were both
regenerate and unregenerate people. This mixed nature of the
Covenant of Grace was justified by a separation between the
external reality and the internal reality of the covenant in supposing
that it was possible to have one without the other. Thus, they
thought, the unconditional nature and effectiveness of the New
Covenant were preserved, since only the substance of the New
Covenant was unconditional and effective; but those who only had
one status in the visible Church could fall and thereby transgress the
New Covenant in which "they were sanctified by the blood of
Christ." However, all these notions were completely foreign to the
New Covenant which, according to biblical terms, explicitly
affirmed the contrary of paedobaptist theology. In fact, the
Scriptures declare that no member of the New Covenant can be
deprived of its substance, the latter being nothing less than salvation
in Jesus Christ.[13] The Scriptures do not provide any possibilities of

---

[12] *Ibid.*, p. 199. The italics are in the original since Blake is quoting another
theologian.

[13] The New Covenant cannot be less effective than the Old Covenant. The latter
offered all its blessings to all its members. If all of them were not saved it was
only because salvation was not a part of the blessings that it had to offer. In the
same way, the New Covenant offers all its blessings to all its members; these
blessings specifically regard salvation. If a member of the New Covenant was not
saved, it would, therefore, be less effective than the Old Covenant since, contrary
to the Old, it could not guarantee all that it offers. John Owen writes: "Those with
whom the Old Covenant was made were all of them actual partakers of the
benefits of it; and if they are not so with whom the new is made, it comes short of
the old in efficacy, and may be utterly frustrated." *An Exposition of Hebrews 8:6-
13*, p. 303.

being visibly in the New Covenant without participating effectively in its substance.

1.2. The Substance of the New Covenant

Not only did the newness of the New Covenant consist in its unconditional nature, but also in that all its members would participate in the substance of the Covenant of Grace: "No longer will they teach their neighbour, or say to one another, 'Know the Lord,' because they will all know me, from the least of them to the greatest," declares the Lord. (Jer. 31.34). In this regard, John (the Baptist) Owen writes: "Where there is not some degree of saving knowledge, there no interest in the New Covenant can be pretended."[14]

The Scriptures declare that the substance of the New Covenant can be summarized in three blessings: the Law written on the heart (regeneration), the personal and saving knowledge of God and the forgiveness of sins which constitute the basis of the other two blessings and of the whole New Covenant (" כִּיאֶסְלַחחלַעֲוֹנָם," "because I will forgive their sin"). God takes great care in saying that this substance would not be the inheritance of only some amongst his people, but of all his people inclusively: "because they will all know me, from the least of them to the greatest," declares the Lord." How, when facing such affirmations, could one insert a dichotomy in the New Covenant by declaring that only a part of its members would inherit its substance while another part would content itself with external blessings that are not mentioned anywhere in the Scriptures?

Let us finish with a quote from theologian Benjamin Keach, where which he stands in awe before the unconditional nature and the effectiveness of the blessings that the New Covenant gives to all its members:

> It is a Full Covenant; because in it there is the Mediators Fullness Communicated to all such that are united to him as the

---

[14] *Ibid.*, p. 299.

effects thereof, 'tis not a Creature-Fullness that is in Christ; no, but the Fullness of God: For it pleased the Father that in him all Fullness should dwell; — in him dwelleth the Fullness of the God-head Bodily: The Fullness of the God-head dwells as truly in the Son, as in the Father; and of his Fullness do all Believers partake, Of his Fullness all we receive, and Grace for Grace.

1. Therefore in this Covenant, we do not only receive Light, but the Fullness of Light.

2. Not only Life, but the Fullness of Life, because Christ is our Life whom we receive in this Covenant.

3. Not only Strength, but the Fullness of Strength; The Lord is the Strength of my heart, and my Portion forever.

4. Not only Pardon of Sin, but Fullness of Pardon; or, the Fullest Pardon, complete Pardon.

5. Not only Righteousness, but the Fullness of Righteousness; perfect and complete Righteousness, and you are complete in him.

6. Not only Peace, but the Fullness of Peace; Peace that passes all understanding.

7. Not only Beauty, but the Fullness of Beauty; for it was perfect, thro' my Comeliness which I put upon thee, saith the Lord God.

8. Not only knowledge, but the Fullness of knowledge; And ye also are Full of all goodness, filled with all knowledge, &c.
The parts may be weak, yet where Christ dwells or hath taken possession of the heart, there the Soul hath a Fullness of Spiritual knowledge: Our Vessels may be full though' but small.

9. Not only Joy, but the Fullness of Joy.[15]

---

[15] Benjamin Keach, *The Display of Glorious Grace*, p. 197-98.

Conclusion

We now find ourselves at the end of our study. Our initial objective was to bring out the differences between paedobaptist covenant theology in the seventeenth century and that of their Baptist contemporaries. We put forth the hypothesis that covenant theology was the most fundamental distinction between these two groups and that the only way to understand the doctrinal and practical differences between the two is by understanding their respective federalisms. We believe that we have demonstrated this.

At the end of this work, we are faced with a marked impression, to be specific, that Presbyterian federalism was an artificial construction developed to justify an end: paedobaptism. We do not think that this laborious theology was the result of a rigorous and disinterested application of hermeneutical principles. We rather believe that it was the consequence of an age-old practice, which became the ultimate instrument of social uniformity in Christendom and which was inherited by the Reformed Church, namely, paedobaptism.[1] Paedobaptism was the arrival point of Presbyterian federalism because it was its starting point. We do not purport that paedobaptists were dishonest, but, at the very least, that they were profoundly influenced by their tradition.

Intolerance, sometimes violent, towards those who rejected both the paedobaptist practice and the doctrine indicates a great difficulty in questioning the foundation of reformed theology. Some Anabaptists, in the 16th century, attacked paedobaptism, but they were quickly executed and their successors later rejected the whole reformed way of thinking. Then, the arrival of the Baptists in the seventeenth century in England considerably challenged the foundations of paedobaptist reformed theology. The Baptists, benefiting from a more favourable context, were able to perform an

---

[1] Cf. Leonard Verduin, *The Anatomy of A Hybrid: A Study in Church-State Relationships*, Grand Rapids, Eerdmans, 1976, 274 p.

in depth analysis of Presbyterian federalism and exposed what, to them, appeared to be its faults. They criticized very rigorously the Presbyterians' covenant theology, on which the doctrines of the Church and of baptism rested. In no way did the Baptists reject reformed theology; however, they reformed its foundations in order to give the edifice a more solid base and much greater harmony with the doctrines of the grace of God.

The Baptist theology was relatively well preserved until the twentieth century where many Baptist churches slid into Arminianism and Dispensationalism. The writings and thought of the first Baptist theologians were almost forgotten. But in the last decades, more and more Baptists are rediscovering their reformed heritage and also their Baptist particularities. This is how covenant theology found itself once again at the center of the dialogue between the Baptists and the Presbyterians. We wanted, in unearthing these old seventeenth-century discussions, to contribute to the present dialogue. We hope to have helped clarify the distinct understandings of the covenants as well as the issues surrounding these questions.

Soli Deo Gloria

Bibliography

Primary Sources

A Confession of Faith, of the Severall Congregations or Churches of Christ in London, which are commonly (though unjustly) called Anabaptists, The second Impression corrected and enlarged, London, Printed by Matth. Simmons, 1646.

Ames, William, *The Marrow of Theology*, Grand Rapids, Baker, 1997 (1629), 353 p.

Ball, John, *A Treatise of the Covenant of Grace*, Dingwall, Peter and Rachel Reynolds, 2006 (1645), 350 p.

Beddome, Benjamin, *A Scriptural Exposition of the Baptist Catechism*, Birmingham, Solid Ground Christian Books, 2006 (1776), 209 p.

Blake, Thomas, *The Birth Priviledge; or Covenant Holinesse of Beleevers and their Issue in the Time of the Gospel*, London, Printed by G.M. for Tho. Underhill, 1643, 33 p.

_____, *Vindiciae Foederis; or A Treatise of the Covenant of God Entered With Man-Kinde, In the Severa Kindes and Degrees of it*, London, Printed for Abel Roper, 1653, 488 p.

Bolton, Samuel, *The True Bounds of Christian Freedom*, Carlisle, The Banner of Truth Trust, 1964 (1645), 224 p.

Boston, Thomas, *A View of the Covenant of Grace From the Sacred Records*, Glasgow, Printed by Robert and Thomas Duncan, 1770 (1742), 407 p.

Bulkeley, Peter, *The Gospel Covenant; or The Covenant of Grace Opened*, London, Printed by M.S. for Benjamin Allen, 1646, 383 p.

Bunyan, John, "The Doctrine of the Law and Grace Unfolded," *The Works of John Bunyan*, Carlisle, Banner of Truth Trust, 1991, volume 1, p. 492-575

Burgess, Anthony, *Vindicie Legis: or, A Vindication of the Morall Law and the Covenants*, London, 1643.

Calvin, Jean, *Institution de la religion chrétienne*, Aix-en-Provence, Kerygma & Excelsis, 2009, 1515 p.

_____, *Commentaries on the Epistle to the Hebrews*, Grand Rapids, Baker, 1999 (1549), 448 p.

Coxe, Nehemiah, "A Discourse of the Covenants that God made with men before the Law," *Covenant Theology: From Adam to Christ*, Palmdale, Reformed Baptist Academic Press, 2005 (1681), p. 25-140.

Dickson, David, *Truth's Victory Over Error*, Edinburgh, Printed by John Reid, 1684, 131 p.

Ferris, Ebenezer, *A Reply to the General Arguments Brought in Favour of Infant Baptism*, New York, Anderson, 1774, 107 p.

Goodwin, Thomas, "A Discourse of Election" *The Works of Thomas Goodwin*, Volume 9, Grand Rapids, Reformation Heritage Books, 2006 (1682), p. 426-498.

Grantham, Thomas, *Truth and Peace or the Last and most Friendly Debate Concerning Infant Baptism*, London, Printed for the Author, 1689, 91 p.

Hutchinson, Edward, *A Treatise Concerning the Covenant and Baptism*, London, Printed for Francis Smith, 1676, 108 p.

_____, *Animadversions Upon a Late Book, Intituled, Infant Baptism From Heaven and not of Men, In Answer to Mr. Henry Danvers his Treatise of Baptism*, 56 p.

_____, *Some Short Questions and Answers for the Younger Sort*, London, Printed for Francis Smith, 1676.

Keach, Benjamin, *The Everlasting Covenant*, London, Printed for H. Barnard, 1693, 44 p.

_____, *The Display of Glorious Grace: Or, The Covenant of Peace Opened. In Fourteen Sermons*, London, Printed by S. Bridge, 1698, 304 p.

La confession de foi baptiste de Londres de 1689, Québec, Association d'Églises réformées baptistes du Québec, 2007, 63 p.

Lawrence, Henry, *Of Baptism*, London, Printed by F. Macock, 1659 (1646), 187 p.

Olevianus, Caspar. *A Firm Foundation: An Aid to Interpreting the Heidelberg Catechism*, Grand Rapids, Baker, 1995, 132 p.

Owen, John, "The Doctrine of Justification by Faith" *The Works of John Owen,* volume 5, Carlisle, The Banner of Truth Trust, 1968 (1677), p. 1-400.

_____, "The Death of Death in the Death of Christ" *The Works of John Owen,* volume 10, Carlisle, The Banner of Truth Trust, 1968 (1647), p. 139-428.

_____, "A Review of the True Nature of Schism," *The Works of John Owen,* volume 13, Carlisle, The Banner of Truth Trust, 1967 (1657), p. 207-275.

_____, "Of Infant Baptism and Dipping" *The Works of John Owen,* volume 16, Carlisle, The Banner of Truth Trust, 1968 (1721), p. 258-268.

_____, "An Exposition of Hebrews 8:6-13: Wherein, the nature and differences between the Old and New Covenants is discovered," *Covenant Theology: From Adam to Christ*, Palmdale, Reformed Baptist Academic Press, 2005, p. 151-312.

_____, *An Exposition of the Epistle to the Hebrews*, Carlisle, The Banner of Truth Trust, 1991, 7 volumes.

Patient, Thomas, *The Doctrine of Baptism, And the Distinction of the Covenants*, London, Printed by Henry Hills, 1654. Available at: http://victorian.fortunecity.com/dadd/464/patient.html

Petto, Samuel, *The Great Mystery of the Covenant of Grace*, Stoke-on-Trent, Tentmaker Publications, 2007 (1820), 251 p.

_____, *Infant Baptism of Christ's Appointment*, London, Printed for Edward Giles, 1687, 97 p.

_____, *Infant-Baptism Vindicated from the Exceptions of Mr. Thomas Grantham*, London, Printed by T.S. for Ed. Giles, 1691, 18 p.

Renihan, James M. (ed.), *True Confessions: Baptist Documents in the Reformed Family*, Owensboro, Reformed Baptist Academic Press, 2004, 291 p.

Renihan, Mike (ed.), *A Confession of Faith, 1677*, Auburn, B & R Press, 142 p.

Ritor, Andrew, *A Treatise of the Vanity of Childish-Baptisme*, London, 1642, 32 p.

Rollock, Robert, *A Treatise of our Effectual Calling*, Harvard College Library, 1828 (1597), 566 p. Available at:

http://books.google.ca/books?id=LugYAAAAYAAJ&lpg=PA 29&ots=baBLshms1E&dq=A%20Treatise%20of%20our%20 Effectual%20Callin&hl=fr&pg=PP1

Spilsbury, John, *A Treatise Concerning the Lawfull Subject of Baptisme*, London, By me J.S., 1643, 44 p.

The Confession of Faith, of those Churches which are commonly (though falsly) called Anabaptists, London, 1644.

Turretin, Francis, *Intitutes of Elenctic Theology*, Phillipsburg, P&R, 1992 (1696), 3 volumes.

Vincent, Thomas, *The Shorter Catechism Explained form Scripture*, Carlisle, The Banner of Truth Trust, 1980 (1674), 282 p.

Witsius, Herman, *The Economy of the Covenants Between God and Man*, Kingsburg CA, den Dulk Christian Foundation, 1990 (réimprimé), 2 volumes.

Secondary Sources

Alumni Cantabrigienses, Cambridge University Press, 10 volumes, 1922–1958.

Asselt, Willem J. van, *The Federal Theology of Johannes Cocceius: (1603-1669)*, Boston, Brill, 2001, 360 p.

Barcellos, Richard C., *In Defense of the Decalogue: A Critique of New Covenant Theology*, Enumclaw, WinePress, 2001, 117 p.

_____, "John Owen and New Covenant Theology," *Covenant Theology: From Adam to Christ*, Palmdale, Reformed Baptist Academic Press, 2005, p. 317-354.

_____, *The Family Tree of Reformed Biblical Theology: Geerhardus Vos and John Owen, Their Methods of and Contributions to the Articulation of Redemptive History*, Owensboro, Reformed Baptist Academic Press, 2010, 324 p.

Beeke, Joel R. & Pederson, Randall J., *Meet the Puritans*, Grand Rapids, Reformation Heritage Books, 2006, 896 p.

Benedict, David, *A General History of the Baptist Denomination in America and Other Parts of the World*, New York, Lewis Colby and Company, 1850, 970 p.

Bierma, Lyle, D., *The Covenant Theology of Caspar Olevianus*, Grand Rapids, Reformation Heritage Books, 2005, 203 p.

Bremer, Francis J., *Puritanism: A Very Short Introduction*, Oxford, Oxford University Press, 2009, 122 p.

Briggs, J.H.Y., "F.A. Cox of Hackney," *Baptist Quarterly*, Vol 38, N° 8, 2000, p. 392-411.

Bromiley, G.W. (ed.), *Zwingli and Bullinger,* Louisville, WJKP, 1953, 364 p.

Brown, Michael, *Christ and the Condition: The Covenant Theology of Samuel Petto (1624-1711)*, Grand Rapids, Reformation Heritage Books, 2012, 139 p.

Bruce, F. F., *The Epistle to the Hebrews, Revised,* NICNT, Grand Rapids, Eerdmans, 1990, 426 p.

Collins, George Norman MacLeod, "Federal Theology," *Evangelical Dictionary of Theology* (2nd edition), Grand Rapids, Baker, 2001, p. 444-445

Conner, Alan, *Covenant Children Today: Physical or Spiritual?*, Owensboro, Reformed Baptist Academic Press, 2007, 122 p.

Dictionary of National Biography, London, Smith, Elder & Co., 1885-1900, 63 volumes.

Duncan, Ligon (ed.), *The Westminster Confession into the 21st Century*, Ross-shire, Mentor, 2003-2009, 3 volumes.

_____, "Recent Objections to Covenant Theology: A Description, Evaluation and Response," *The Westminster Confession into the 21st Century*, vol. 3, Ross-shire, Mentor, 2009 p. 467-500.

_____, *Covenant Theology; The Abrahamic Covenant—Covenant Signs, Covenant Sign Implications*, 12 two-hour lectures from the RTS Covenant Theology Course. Available at:

http://www.fpcjackson.org/resources/apologetics/Covenant%20Theology%20&%20Justification/index.htm

Ellingworth, Paul, *The Epistle to the Hebrews*, NIGTC, Grand Rapids, Eerdmans, 1993, 764 p.

Estelle, Bryan D., J.V. Fesko and David VanDrunen, eds., *The Law Is Not Of Faith: Essays on Works and Grace in the Mosaic Covenant*, Phillipsburg, P&R, 2009, 358 p.

Favre, Olivier, *Le bon fondement*, Pully, Éditions Repères, 2007, 295 p.

Ferguson, Sinclair B., *John Owen on the Christian Life*, Carlisle, The Banner of Truth Trust, 1987, 297 p.

Fiddes, Paul S., *Tracks and Traces, Baptist Identity in Church and Theology*, Eugene OR, Wipf & Stock, 2003, 305 p.

Fisher, James, *Exposition of the Shorter Catechism*, Stoke-on-Trent, Tentmaker Publications, 1998 (1753), 477 p.

Fowler, Stanley K., *More than a Symbol, The British Baptist Recovery of Baptismal Sacramentalism*, Eugene OR, Wipf & Stock, 2002, 276 p.

Gentry, Peter J. & Stephen J. Wellum, *Kingdom Through Covenant: A Biblical-Theological Understanding of the Covenants*, Wheaton, Crossway, 2012, 848 p.

George, Timothy, "Baptists and the Westminster Confession," *The Westminster Confession into the 21st Century*, vol. 1, Ross-shire, Mentor, 2003, p. 145-159.

Gribben, Crawford, *The early Irish Baptists*, Escondido, The Institute of Reformed Baptist Studies, March 17 2008. Available at: http://www.reformedbaptistinstitute.org/?p=60

Hall, David W. & Peter A. Lillback, eds., *Theological Guide to Calvin's Institutes*, Philipsburg, P&R, 2008, 506 p.

Haykin, Michael A.G., *Rediscovering our English Baptist Heritage, Kiffin, Knollys ans Keach*, Leeds, Reformation Today Trust, 1996, 125 p.

Hodge, A.A., *The Confession of Faith*, Carlisle, The Banner of Truth Trust, 1958, 404 p.

Horton, Michael, *God of Promise, Introducing Covenant Theology*, Grand Rapids, Baker, 2006, 204 p.

Hughes, Philip E., *A Commentary on the Epistle to the Hebrews*, Grand Rapids, Eerdmans, 1977, 623 p.

Ivimey, Joseph, *A History of the English Baptists*, London, Printed by Burditt and Morris, 1811, 572 p.

Jewett, Paul K., *Infant Baptism & the Covenant of Grace*, Grand Rapids, Eerdmans, 1978, 254 p.

Johnson, Jeffrey D., *The Fatal Flaw of the Theology Behind Infant Baptism*, Free Grace Press, 2010, 268 p.

Karlberg, Mark W., *Covenant Theology in Reformed Perspective*, Eugene OR, Wipf and Stock Publishers, 2000, 419 p.

Kistemaker, Simon J., *Exposition of the Epistle to the Hebrews*, New Testament Commentary, Grand Rapids, Baker, 1984, 464 p.

Kingdon, David, *Children of Abraham*, Sussex, Carey Publications, 1973, 105 p.

Macleod, Donald, *A Faith to Live by, Christian Teaching That Makes a Difference*, Ross-shire, Mentor, 1998, 309 p.

Malone, Fred, *The Baptism of Disciples Alone*, Cape Coral, Founders Press, 2003, 284 p.

_____, *Covenant Theology for Baptists*, unpublished course notes.

McBeth, H. Leon, *The Baptist Heritage, Four Centuries of Baptist Witness*, Nashville, Broadman Press, 1987, 850 p.

McKim, Donald K., *The Westminster Handbook to Reformed Theology*, Louisville, WJKP, 2001, 243 p.

Muller, Richard A., *Post-Reformation Reformed Dogmatics*, Grand Rapids, Baker, 1993, 4 volumes.

_____, *Dictionary of Latin and Greek Theological Terms*, Grand Rapids, Baker, 1985, 340 p.

Murray, John, *Collected Writings,* Carlisle, The Banner of Truth, 1976, 4 Volumes.

_____, *The Covenant of Grace*, Phillipsburg, P&R, 1953, 32 p.

Naylor, Peter, *Calvinism, Communion and the Baptists, A Study of English Calvinistic Baptists form the Late 1600s to the Early 1800s*, Eugene OR, Wipf & Stock, 2003, 265 p.

Nettles, Thomas J., "Baptist View: Baptism as a Symbol of Christ's Saving Work," *Understanding Four Views on Baptism*, Grand Rapids, Zondervan, 2007, p. 25-41.

Nichols, Greg, *The Solemn Promises of Salvation: God's Covenants and the Covenant of Grace*, Teaching notes (unpublished).

_____, *Covenant Theology: A Reformed and Baptistic Perspective on God's Covenants*, Birmingham, Solid Ground Christian Books, 2011, 365 p

Osterhaven, M. Eugene, "Covenant Theology," *Evangelical Dictionary of Theology* (2nd edition), Grand Rapids, Baker, 2001, p. 301-303

Oxford English Dictionary

Packer, J.I., *Introduction: On Covenant Theology*. Available at:

http://gospelpedlar.com/articles/Bible/cov_theo.html

Parker, T.H.L. (ed.), *English Reformers*, Louisville, WJKP, 1966, 360 p.

Pratt Jr., Richard L., "Reformed View: Baptism as a Sacrament of the Covenant," *Understanding Four Views on Baptism*, Grand Rapids, Zondervan, 2007, p. 59-72.

Renihan, James M., *Edification and Beauty: The Practical Ecclesiology of the English Particular Baptists, 1675-1705*, Eugene OR, Wipf & Stock, 2009, 232 p.

_____, "An Excellent and Judicious Divine: Nehemiah Coxe," *Covenant Theology: From Adam to Christ*, Palmdale, Reformed Baptist Academic Press, 2005, p. 7-24

Riker, D.B., *A Catholic Reformed Theologian: Federalism and Baptism in the Thought of Benjamin Keach, 1640-1704*, Eugene OR, Wipf & Stock, 2009, 257 p.

Robertson O. Palmer, *The Christ of the Covenants,* Phillipsburg, R&R, 1980, 308 p.

_____, *The Christ of the Prophets*, Phillipsburg, P&R, 2004, 553 p.

_____, *The Israel of God*, New Jersey, P&R, 2000, 204 p.

Rohr, John Von, *The Covenant of Grace in Puritan Thought*, Atlanta, Scholars Press, 1986, 226 p.

Schreiner, Thomas R. & WRIGHT Shawn D., eds., *Believer's Baptism, Sign of the New Covenant in Christ*, Nashville, B&H Publishing Group, 2006, 364 p.

Shaff, Philip, *The Creeds of Christendom*, 6th edition, Grand Rapids, Baker, 1993, 3 volumes.

Shaw, Robert, *An Exposition of the Westminster Confession of Faith*, Ross-shire, Christian Focus, 1998, 398 p.

Smith, Paul, *The Westminster Confession: Enjoying God Forever*, Chicago, Moody Press, 237 p.

Sproul, R.C., *Truths We Confess, A Layman's Guide to the Westminster Confession of Faith*, Phillipsburg, P&R, 2006, 3 volumes.

Spurgeon, Charles Haddon, *The Sermons of Rev. C.H. Spurgeon of London*, 9th Series, New York, Robert Carter & Brothers, 1883, 510 p.

Verduin, Leonard, *The Anatomy of A Hybrid: A Study in Church-State Relationships*, Grand Rapids, Eerdmans, 1976, 274 p.

Vos, Johannes G., *The Westminster Larger Catechism*, Phillipsburg, P&R, 2002, 614 p.

Waldron, Samuel E., *A Modern Exposition of the 1689 Baptist Confession of Faith*, Webster, Evangelical Press, 1989, 490 p.

_____, *Biblical Baptism, A Reformed Defense of Believers Baptism*, Grand Rapids, Truth For Eternity Ministries, 1998, 80 p.

_____ & Richard C. Barcellos, *A Reformed Baptist Manifesto, The New Covenant Constitution of the Church*, Palmdale, Reformed Baptist Academic Press, 2004, 113 p.

Wellum, Stephen J., "Baptism and the Relationship Between the Covenants," *Believer's Baptism, Sign of the New Covenant in Christ*, Nashville, B&H Publishing Group, 2006, p. 97-161.

Williamson, G.I., *The Westminster Confession of Faith for Study Classes, 2nd edition*, Phillipsburg, P&R, 2004 (1964), 409 p.

_____, *The Heidelberg Catechism, A Study Guide*, Phillipsburg, P&R, 1993, 241 p.

Williamson, J.R., *From the Garden of Eden to the Glory of Heaven*, Amityville, Calvary Press, 2008, 240 p.

Wright, Shawn D., "Baptism and the Logic of Reformed Paedobaptists," *Believers's Baptism, Sign of the New Covenant in Christ*, Nashville, B&H Publishing Group, 2006, p. 207-255.

Zepp, Renfred Errol, *Covenant Theology From the Perspective of Two Puritans*, Charlotte, Reformed Theological Seminary, 2009, 81 p.